ANARCHY AND APATHY

ANARCHY AND APATHY

Student Unrest 1968-70

BY

MARGARET ANNE ROOKE

HAMISH HAMILTON

LONDON

First published in Great Britain 1971
by Hamish Hamilton Ltd
90 *Great Russell Street London WC*1

Copyright © 1971 *by Margaret Anne Rooke*

SBN 241 02070 0

Printed in Great Britain
by Ebenezer Baylis and Son Limited
The Trinity Press, Worcester, and London

Contents

Preface

I wish to thank those officials of students' unions who have answered my enquiries. These are the president of Manchester University students' union, the president of Bath University students' union, the president of University College, London, students' union, the president of Warwick University students' union and the secretary of Birmingham University guild of undergraduates. The other universities which I asked for statistical information did not reply.

This book is not intended to be a comprehensive account of all disturbances. It is a general outline of them as a whole. Let no one complain because some commotion at his institution has been omitted.

I have omitted the names of those who have stated that they do not wish to receive any personalized fame as a result of their activities.

I wish to thank my husband for his encouragement and assistance and Mrs Joyce Maxwell for typing up my manuscript.

M.A.R.
January 1971

I

Introduction

OVER THE past two or three years student disturbances in Britain have attracted much attention from the public. They have differed from previous demonstrations of student opinion in their scale, organization and purpose and have impressed themselves forcibly on the public's consciousness. For the first time in the history of British universities, teaching and administration have been deliberately and violently disrupted while the extra-curricular activities of some students resulted in imprisonment. It is not student misbehaviour that is novel but the forms it takes. Formerly, brawling stopped at the lecture-room door; it is its intrusion into the arena of intellectual debate that is the fundamental and striking change.

This book is being written to answer four questions put by the public. These questions have been asked in countless forms and with varying degrees of exasperation. They have been asked in the Press, on the television and in private conversation. 'How long is this hideous and expensive pantomime going to continue?' was one of the typical manifestations of angry public bewilderment in the *Evening Standard*. In essentials the questions asked are: 'What exactly is going on in our universities and colleges?', 'Why don't the moderates stop it?', 'Why don't the authorities stop it?', and 'Why is it happening anyway?'

Innumerable explanations have already been offered. The Right wing of the Conservative Party believes firmly that university disruption is organized by the agents of the Great Red Plot; its Monday Club holds closed conferences on 'Internal Subversion'. The Chairman of the National Sheepbreeders' Association has suggested that student unrest may be caused by a lack of vitamins and that more meat would remedy this. Professor Richard Hoggart has claimed that these students are acting out the end of the protestant ethic. A lecturer at a MENSA function asserted that the troubles were caused by the too-early marriages of modern dons and students; Professor Northcote Parkinson told an audience that it was the fault of women for demanding emancipation and evading control by their husbands for—so his argument ran—in so doing they in their turn lost control over their children. The Liberal Party spokesman for education has claimed that the student protesters are young idealists exposing the anti-democratic nature of our society; a similarly charitable view is taken by many clergy who suppose that some religious feeling is beneath the political disturbances. Predictably the Russian Government commented on 'the turbulent upsurge' of youth in the West and called it an indication of the decay of capitalism. The Labour Minister of Education who actually had to deal with the situation made several speeches on 'the thugs of the academic world' and 'the wreckers of society'.

However, none of these theories is satisfactory. For most no evidence whatsoever has been offered. Most reflected the personal preoccupations of their holders. The bewildering variety and complexity of student disturbance make an entirely simple explanation improbable. This variety and complexity reflect the variety and complexity of British society. In Britain even 'revolution' is conservative. The extraordinary mixture of apparent causes of student disturbance makes the view that there is some sinister force at work almost untenable. Vietnam, the Welsh language, squatters, Biafra, college bus-services, Rhodesia, lodgings, Greece, refectory prices and Ireland have all made their contribution.

The period covered by this study is the two years from October 1968 to August 1970. This is not because it is supposed that disturbances did not take place before. It is because the October 27 Vietnam March focussed public attention on what is called student protest. This demonstration marked the transition of student unrest from the occasional to the endemic state.

The first serious disturbance came in 1967 at the London School of Economics when the precedent of the 'sit-in' or 'occupation' was established by 1,000 students who thus obtained the abandonment of disciplinary action against two of their colleagues. The following academic year 1967–8 saw further incidents, mostly brief and isolated. At Sussex University, in February 1968, red paint was thrown at an official of the United States embassy. Both Hornsey and Guildford Schools of Art had long sit-ins. An attempt was made to start a 'free university' at Bristol University. An attempt had, indeed, been made to found an anti-university at London; unsupported by public funds it crumbled.

At Leeds in June 1968 a short sit-in was held against the decision of the university not to investigate allegations of 'political spying' on students. At Hull one student tore up his degree papers and several hundred of his colleagues demonstrated in support of him—though not to the extent of following his example.

The precedent of denying the right of free speech to politicians visiting universities became established. 'To demonstrate' acquired the secondary meaning, 'to shout down'. Mr. Harold Wilson, then Prime Minister, and Mr. Dennis Healey, then Minister of Defence, found intolerant receptions at Oxbridge. While protecting Mrs. Wilson a policeman was injured so badly that he had to leave the police force. 'To demonstrate' was, indeed, acquiring also the meaning 'to brawl with the police'. At both the March and July Vietnam demonstrations in 1968 more police were injured than demonstrators. One policeman was injured for life.

However, the visiting politician whose arrival at an institution was most likely to give rise to disturbance was not a member of the government nor even of the shadow cabinet. This was Mr. Enoch Powell, Conservative Member of Parliament for Wolverhampton South-West.

This M.P. requires some description. He had been a professor of classics and a brigadier. After the war he had risen inside the Conservative Party and had enjoyed office. During the party's time in opposition he had been shadow Minister of Defence. A speech he made in the spring of 1968 removed him from the shadow cabinet.

In this speech he called for the stricter limitation of coloured immigration. He produced some dubious statistics and retailed some even more dubious anecdotes. His speech was enlivened by such phrases as 'rivers of blood' and 'grinning piccaninnies'. There was an immediate reaction from almost everyone able to read a newspaper—and the overwhelming majority of people supported his views. He was widely hailed as 'the man of the century'.

The liberal and articulate minority was horrified. It clung to the Race Relations Act and embarked on a campaign to impress the facts of the situation on the public. The actual numbers of the immigrant communities and their vital contribution to the economic welfare of the country were emphasized by Labour, Liberal and Conservative spokesmen with such success that Mr. Powell eventually suggested that their figures were faked by the civil service. He was unable to produce the central figure of one of his anecdotes—the old lady through whose door excrement was pushed —and was finally driven to say, in effect, that the story was so widely known and believed that it must have some basis in fact. At last, according to a *Daily Telegraph* poll, support for Mr. Powell sank below the 50 per cent line—though not before irreparable harm had been done. Even his most ardent critics had been pushed to appease popular feeling. The Labour M.P. in the adjoining constituency who had wanted to invoke the Race Relations Act against him was compelled to ask that no more worker vouchers should be given to immigrants wishing to settle in Wolverhampton.

It seemed as if the liberal consensus was endangered, that the tolerance which permeated British politics and society was being strained and that a genuine Right on the Continental model was emerging. Mr. Powell brought the submerged hysteria of millions to the surface and stirred people as they had not been stirred for years. He also provided a focus of hysteria for the Left and aroused an intensity of hatred and bitterness that startled even those who felt it. Mr. Powell's popularity encouraged the authoritarian tendencies of the Left, both the moderate and the extreme. The workers had finally taken political action and marched to the House of Commons in support of Mr. Powell. It became even more difficult for the Left to claim that 'the people' should get its way. The advocates of 'participation' of the Labour and Liberal parties were thus at a loss. The Conservative Party was split between the leadership and the bulk of M.P.s on the one hand and the grassroots Tories on the other. It was alleged, with truth, that the parties were out of touch with the people. There was a frightening gulf between the educated and the uneducated and semi-educated.

This issue which released such passion gave both major parties an injection of fanaticism. Some of the extreme Left of the Labour Party were prepared to deny Mr. Powell free speech; and some of the Conservative Party felt that he erred on the side of moderation. The weight of opinion of both parties lay in the centre; but the margin of safety that was maintained by those who were determined never to yield to the forces released by Mr. Powell, and equally determined to ensure that he was free to express his views, seemed sometimes dangerously slender. In the event the liberal consensus was preserved by the moderation of most of those with power and the apathy of most of those without it.

Thus, by the summer of 1968 most of those inside universities were, on one issue at least, deeply opposed to most of those outside them. The visit of Mr. Powell to Essex University resulted in an attempt by the university to discipline three students—and a thousand students who had not taken part in the incident met to protest. They thus set a precedent of providing retroactive sanction for acts in which they had not taken part and which they would not have attended a meeting to approve beforehand. Mr. Powell's difficulties were shared by Major Patrick Wall, Conservative M.P. for Haltemprice; his visit to Leeds University ended in a disturbance during the course of which he was spat at and his wife was kicked. Episodes of this nature provided immense publicity for their central figures.

Before describing in detail the series of events in British universities from the summer of 1968, it is necessary to outline the origin and development of these institutions.

The usual definition of a university is an institution or group in which knowledge is both extended and imparted. Universities have, of course, been in existence since the Greek city-states arrived at full consciousness. They were not institutions with labels but gatherings round some man or men considered to be wiser than others. Ionia produced the first of these seekers after knowledge. The greatest was Socrates. He did not, however, suppose that he was extending knowledge but drawing it out of the depths of the mind. His pupil and successor, Plato, was not so exclusively factual in his approach; he thought that when a certain degree of knowledge had been attained revelation would give complete understanding. The search for knowledge was touched with mysticism—and this tradition continued through the classical and Christian periods.

Centres of learning developed in the cities of the Roman Empire and young men attended them less in the pursuit of wisdom than in the pursuit of worldly success. Empires need bureaucrats. Literacy and numeracy were indispensable. Many Athenians had acquired an education so that in the courts, where a man was not allowed to hire another to represent him, he could defend his interests. On the larger scale of the Roman Empire this tendency was carried to its logical conclusion. There were also considerations that induced scholars to group together rather than ponder in isolation; in a world where every book had to be copied out by hand scholars needed to congregate round libraries, and the destruction of one of these was a major disaster. This entire development was much more clearly shown in China where for centuries written examinations were taken to secure admission to the ranks of the ruling mandarins. As one complacently began a poem: 'The world cheats those who cannot read./I happily have mastered script and pen.'

The search for truth has always been at least touched and often governed by revelation on the one hand and utilitarianism on the other, even in classical times when the official state religion was not taken seriously except in public ceremonials.

The Christian era saw the strengthening of the influence of both revelation and utilitarianism. For these reasons the modern universities in embryo became centres of the transmission of faith as well as fact. There were obvious practical reasons. The chaos of the Dark Ages was hardly the time to challenge accepted opinion. The duty of the educated was to assist and justify law and order rather than to risk subverting them. It is true that facts and interpretations were widely exchanged and passionately discussed but the primary reason for the development of universities from the eleventh century onwards was the need of a Europe emerging from barbarism for men to run it. If they had not been forthcoming the developing national and local states would have gone the way of Charlemagne's empire which had scarcely survived him. For a royal writ to be valid in each village there had to be someone able to read it. This was usually, of course, the priest, for laws were publicized by being read from the pulpit. Education was heavily influenced at all levels by the Church. Speculation was only allowed within the confines of the Christian faith, and the greatest work to come from the University of Paris in the Middle Ages was

St. Thomas Aquinas' *Summa Theologica* which was a compilation of all knowledge as he saw it rather than a venture into its extension. He stated explicitly that where fact and faith conflicted the latter should take precedence. There was no scientific enquiry or observation in his book. Empirically verifiable and regularly verified fact was scarcely touched in universities. Even medicine had to be taught from received belief in many places. St. Thomas Aquinas was fortunate to have access to the works of Aristotle for until 1210 they had been denounced as heretical. Education and the Church were firmly conservative; the students who brawled never considered attacking the bases of their courses of study. Universities were to a large extent the agents of the civil power and the servants of the Church.

It has been claimed that in Britain there is a long tradition of academic freedom. This is to distort the facts. The British universities—Oxford, founded in 1249, Cambridge, founded in 1284, and St. Andrews, founded in 1411—were restricted like the French, Italian or German ones. These restrictions were of course not felt, as they would be today, as intolerable limitations on freedom. The universities, in so far as they were ever small communities bound together by the pursuit of wisdom, soon developed into thriving components of the lives of the nations of which they were part, and were therefore much influenced by considerations far removed from the search for truth. Henry VIII concocted a petition signed by innumerable academics demanding an enquiry into, and a release from, his first marriage. The Stuarts forced their nominees on colleges. Universities recognized and perpetuated academically irrelevant social distinctions; noble students could wear gold tassels on their academic dress. The religion of the state was expected of all members. It was not until 1870—a dozen years after the publication of Darwin's *The Origin of Species*—that the Test Acts forbidding entrance to all non-Anglicans were repealed; and for centuries after the abolition of the ecclesiastical laws requiring celibacy of the clergy the Fellows of Oxbridge colleges lost their fellowships if they married. The universities were, as even Edmund Burke admitted, no centres of intellectual life. Not a single one of the inventions that brought about the Industrial Revolution owed its genesis to an English university. The Scottish universities and the academies for protestant dissenters were more in touch with this type of enquiry. It was James Watt's examination of Glasgow University's Newcomen steam-engine that led him to develop an improved one. The older English universities, however, stagnated; their use was limited to the provision of qualifications for the sons of the upper and middle classes—and these qualifications were often to provide younger sons with church livings. Fortunately universities were founded at London and Manchester in the nineteenth century.

This stagnation was shared by many foreign universities. The Enlightenment did not owe its impetus to them. As late as 1750 the universities of Paris and Madrid, to name but two, clung firmly to the Ptolemaic view of the universe. In Catholic countries the existence of the *Index* did not help the extension of knowledge.

However, by the second half of the nineteenth century, the universities began to stir. In Germany Hegel's doctrine of thesis and antithesis gained ground—even though he had been in no sense a revolutionary. Ranke, Fichte and Treitschke captured the attention, in their different ways, of the universities of Germany. In Britain, Oxford and Cambridge were fluttered by the winds of change. The extension of education to a larger proportion of the population and the rise in the standards of living of the nation made university education accessible and economically possible for a wider social variety and a greater number of potential students. By the 1890s it was even proposed that women should be admitted.

The real expansion came with what is loosely called the Welfare State. It became the State's moral duty to educate its youthful members to the level of which they were capable. Disputes over this limitation were to become bitter. Large quantities of money were spent on providing scientific facilities for universities; science was overtaking literacy as the cohesive force of the community. The universities became the extenders of knowledge. Modern science demanded the co-ordination and collective use of resources in a way that primitive science had not. Bacon could make his experiments with a chicken and a handful of snow. Lord Rutherford could not. It is an interesting reflection on the conservatism of Oxbridge that a first science degree is officially still a B.A. British life shows a genius for changing the reality without sacrificing the form.

State aid to universities and the proportion it formed of university income increased. So did its financial provision for students. After the Second World War university education became virtually free for all those able to obtain entrance on academic grounds. The arts benefited almost accidentally. Although the State was contributing so much to the universities, these institutions enjoyed considerable autonomy in spending the money. The State's influence though great was indirect.

The universities responded with remarkable vitality. No longer the lazy defenders of mindless conservatism, they plunged to the front not only of scientific but of historical, economic and political research. Marx and Freud appeared on syllabuses and book-lists. New universities were built and acclaimed. It seemed that modern students had little to complain about.

However, the growth of the passion for 'social justice' led to difficulties in the educational field. It was considered an indication of the essential failure of the system that even the provision of free university places had not resulted in the reflection in universities of the social composition of the community. This discrepancy was also apparent in the grammar schools. Equality of opportunity had not resulted in equality of achievement. It was therefore asserted in some quarters that opportunity was being offered unequally. There can be little doubt that many intelligent and well-educated people felt guilty because they enjoyed a possession that most people could not and did not enjoy. They believed that inherited intellectual differences were insufficient to explain social imbalances in the grammar schools and universities. Despite the shortage of teachers the plan to raise the school-leaving age was defended. An energetic battle was started over the retention of the grammar schools. The Labour government was as determined to remove selection by ability as some of the Conservative councils were to retain it. In 1967 almost every local authority in the country fell to the Conservatives owing to the massive apathy of Labour voters. Streaming was attacked; so was the arrangement of pupils in order of scholastic achievement. The immediate and piecemeal application of these policies led to dislocation.

The implementation of such policies coincided with a 'bulge' in the age-group undergoing education. In other words, a larger proportion of a greater number of adolescents hoped to enter university. The government considered it a duty to provide university education for two main groups: those who needed it to earn a chosen living in a calling indispensable to the community; and those who wanted it for non-vocational reasons.

The consequence of these attitudes was a great increase in the number of students in universities and colleges of further and higher education and also an increase in the national proportion of 18- to 21-year-olds in these institutions. There was immense pressure on books, accommodation and staff attention. Unfortunately, the government lacked the money to provide for these growing student numbers the expanded facilities they needed. The exigencies of the balance of payments created an imbalance in the universities.

Thus, in the autumn of 1968 the recommendations of the Robbins Report of 1963 had resulted in the presence of about 400,000 students in institutions of higher education. Slightly over half of these were in universities. The proportion of 18-year-olds starting a degree course had risen by half. The swing from science, caused partly by the selection of university courses for preference rather than profit, and the tripling of sociology undergraduates over the previous five years changed the composition of student communities.

By October 1968 there was already much public annoyance about student disturbances. The *People* began an article with, 'If the word "student" makes you feel sick . . .' All the factors for the disturbances of the following two years were already present.

This study is concerned only with British conditions and events. Although there were student disturbances in other countries and although these were often taken as part of a world-wide student movement the immediate causes of disturbance were different. British commotions were, of course, much less violent than French, German, Japanese or American ones. This country does not have the same tradition of accepted casual violence for ostensibly political reasons. In none of the countries mentioned above would a policeman have said to a Springboks demonstrator, 'Do you come here often?' Sitters-in at Rhodesia House were offered cups of tea—the first time only. Compared to those of other countries British student disturbances were a storm in a teacup.

Each of the four countries mentioned had its own distinctive type of student revolt; it was loyal to its own traditions. In Japan the extreme Left-wing rioters followed the example of the preceding generation. In the 1930s Right-wing fanatics had assassinated ministers. In the past few years Japanese police have gone armed into battle behind banners against students. They have been called on to besiege universities. Students have beaten up people for not sharing their views. Some students established 'people's courts' in universities: one of these so deeply humiliated a professor of electronics for not teaching his subject in a revolutionary way that he committed suicide.

Events in Germany showed a similar reversion to the 1930s. Before 1933 the National Socialist party had been twice as strong in the universities as in the general population. It was probably memories of those times which made the Germans so unsympathetic to disturbances. It was unfortunate for both Germany and Japan that their university systems were untouched by the war in several vital respects.

French student riots were the most dangerous to the preservation of order, for, in May 1968, the students and workers combined. This short-lived coalition shook France. Although the workers soon deserted, student revolt kept some institutions permanently disrupted. At Vincennes a lecturer led her class to find another lecturer and try him before a 'people's assembly'. He was only saved by a group of communist students.

In the United States student revolt was embittered by opposition to the Vietnam war and by the pressures of racial conflict. At Berkeley one student held a professor's arms while another clubbed him in the face. At Cornell students made their claims with the aid of guns. The town of Yap in Dakota was sacked in a 'happening'.

All these countries are like our own in having some claim to be governed by the machinery of representative democracy, and in enjoying a high standard of living and in holding an influential position in the world. However, each nation's student 'protest' has been different. Far from being international, 'protest' conforms to the tradition of the country. Within this group British student 'revolt' was unique in its mildness and absence of deaths. This was attributed by some to the rigorous selection of students and the high staff-student ratio in the universities.

In some countries students had very real causes of complaint. In Monrovia 133 were disciplined for not attending a military parade in honour of the President. In Egypt there were riots because science students feared that examinations were to be made harder to pass and therefore jobs more difficult to obtain; Colonel Nasser claimed the riots were inspired by the Israelis. In Pakistan students objected to the concentration of power in the hands of General Ayub Khan. In Brazil and Mexico they protested against a very real political repression. In the latter country the government asserted that the protesters were paid by the Central Intelligence Agency and Russia. Greece and Italy each produced their student rebels, though in the former country such rebellion was individual rather than collective. In India students rioted because of attempts to have cheating in examinations stopped; for a degree could mean the difference between poverty and affluence. In South Africa students protested peacefully against the excesses of apartheid.

Protest was mild in mild countries. There was an occupation of Copenhagen University. Mr. Holyoake was screamed at in New Zealand. Their revolts, too, were in their own traditions. Religion played a part in some countries.

It can fairly be claimed that because of the differences of alleged cause, course and consequence between one country's student commotions and another's it would be impossible to include several, let alone all of them, in one study. Each community is unique. The only thing all these students have in common is their age-group. The affinities and similarities are often strong but there are also considerable differences.

This study will therefore be confined to the period between the month of the great Vietnam Demonstration of October 27, 1968 and the rejection in August 1970 of the appeals of several Cambridge students against conviction and imprisonment for disrupting a hotel dinner. Certainly, enough happened in those two years. The methods of student protesters spread through the community. There was a walk-out from an army barracks and a sit-in in a navy ship. 'Sit-ins' became part of our vocabulary and 'occupation' acquired an extra meaning. 'Disrupter', too, entered the language. A list of expressions like 'protest', 'rebel', 'march', 'direct action', 'current', 'assembly', 'provocation' and 'confrontation' acquired new connotations. There were sit-ins in pubs and government offices. There were sit-downs in front of business firms. There were boycotts and token boycotts of all types. There were walk-outs and invasions. The universities generated and set this pattern of behaviour. Outside them, however, it was superficial. Students were a small minority even in their own generation and the activists among them a smaller minority still.

These two years deserve some record and analysis and the questions on the first page deserve some answer.

2

The Year of Vietnam

STUDENT DISTURBANCES in the academic year 1968–69 were ostensibly started by the Vietnam issue and their focal point was the London School of Economics.

The Vietnam War had, of course, been going on since 1960. Indeed the area that is now Vietnam has been fought over for a whole generation. The French had struggled hard to keep it. Since 1965 American combatant forces had been helping the South Vietnamese government to keep down the communist insurgents who were being supported and reinforced by the communist government of North Vietnam. In other words the war itself was nothing new but its use as a pretext for civil disturbance in this country was of recent origin.

In March and July 1968 there had been demonstrations and battles with the police over the Vietnam issue. Those involved numbered hundreds rather than thousands but the publicity they received was immense. The sufferings of the Vietnamese drew from a large proportion of the public sympathy for the demonstrators.

Over the summer a great demonstration was planned for October 27. It became apparent that although all those to be at this demonstration were opponents of the war in Vietnam their opposition was so varied in origin and purpose, and in so many cases a secondary motive for their support, that the march would have little moral cohesion. For some the Vietnam war and the passionate opposition it aroused were the eventual solvents of Western capitalism. For some it would provide a momentary release from a sense of malaise. For some the reason for supporting the demonstration was sympathy for the sufferings of the Vietnamese. In so far as these diverse elements and innumerable local groups could be organized they were organized by an already well-known Pakistani revolutionary ex-student at the head of an appropriate committee. It is hardly too much to say that it was partly his efforts that ensured that the gap left in British life by the virtual extinction of the Campaign for Nuclear Disarmament was temporarily filled.

It has often been asked why the disturbances of the year centred round the London School of Economics. This institution rapidly became the best-known college in the country.

The reasons were simple. It had more than 3,000 students and of these a very large proportion were sociology students. About a third of its students were post-graduate—a proportion which the director was determined to maintain. The actual research done at the institution was in a real sense scholastic and factual, but it cannot be denied that sociology can lend itself to interpretation by revelation in a sense that dentistry, say, does not. The graduate section had its own problems. The Chairman of the Governors, Lord Robbins, had introduced year-long post-graduate M.A. and M.Sc. courses which for anyone who had obtained a first degree in the subject demanded comparatively little time and energy. A large proportion of people doing these courses was American. Indeed about one-tenth of the student body was transatlantic in origin.

These 3,000 students were crowded into three buildings in Houghton Street. The ratio of staff to students was abnormally low. There were 600 library seats. There was no space for a common-room for the undergraduates. Indeed almost the only place where a large number of people could meet was the Old Theatre. Since when this was not being used for lectures it was often used for political meetings and for film showings choice of recreation was limited. There were, it is true, many societies such as the Photography one and the Food and Wine one, but there was no extra-political communal feeling. The fact that the School was in a non-residential area meant that students could have no local contacts. It is perhaps fair to say, however, that any local contacts might not have been happy.

The L.S.E. is in Central London and therefore readily accessible by road and rail from all parts of the country. Holborn Tube Station is only a few hundred yards away. A nearby open space for a gathering point is readily available in Lincoln's Inn Fields. L.S.E. is within easy marching distance of Trafalgar Square, Downing Street, University of London Students' Union building and the United States Embassy in Grosvenor Square. Australia House is just opposite the bottom of Houghton Street and Rhodesia House is less than a quarter of a mile away. A television studio is just round one corner and Fleet Street round another, separated from the L.S.E. only by some business firms—and the law-courts. The stars in their courses fought against the prospect of L.S.E.'s not being the centre of disturbance.

The previous year had been very quiet. For much of it the presidency of the students' union had been held by the chairman of the Conservative Association, Mr. Peter Watherston. After the disturbances of the previous year the poll for the presidency had been very low. A sit-in in support of the French student revolt of May 1968 had been brief and had attracted few students. The recommendations of the Minority Report, produced by two Extreme Left-wing students, that the administration of the school should be carried on by a general assembly of 120 staff and 100 students excited little interest. In October 1968 there were four political societies. The Socialist Society numbered about 200. The Labour Club had about 50 members and the Liberal Club about 60. The Conservative Association had 160 supporters. Actual policy in all four groups was, of course, decided by far smaller numbers. In the cases of both the Liberal and Labour Clubs divisions were so deep that no consistent policy was possible. Far larger numbers voted at elections for union office. There were two basic forces at L.S.E. One group wanted stability and one group did not. Both groups had reservoirs of voters in the student body.

It was obviously going to be a difficult year. Sir Eric Ashby, vice-chancellor of Cambridge University, opened it with a public statement on the central purpose of university education and the necessity of maintaining the academic freedom of these institutions from interference whether from Left or Right, whether from the State or from anarchists.

At Lancaster University the president of the students' union boasted in the students' handbook that students had more share in the government of the institution at Lancaster than anywhere else. However, his optimism was short-lived as term began with the boycott of an examination. An examination so early in the term was considered unreasonable.

Attempts were made to avert the coming storm. The National Union of Students and the committee of vice-chancellors signed an agreement providing for a large measure of student representation. Since there was no machinery for enforcing these provisions and since neither group had any influence at local level this was ineffective. In any case the militant minorities in universities were hardly likely to feel bound by any such agreement. This agreement made it clear that in the view of the N.U.S. academic decisions were the right and responsibility of the teaching staff. It was the target of criticism from both the public and the more demanding students. The Revolutionary Students' Alliance and the Revolutionary Socialist Students' Federation condemned it. The president of Kent University students' union said that he had not expected much anyway. At Kent students were demanding a voice in the selection of a new vice-chancellor.

One vice-chancellor had already had a foretaste of what was to come. Sir Hugh Robson had been delivering his yearly address to Sheffield's new undergraduates when a few dozen of the Socialist Society burst in and demanded a discussion on subjects selected by them. The choice was put to those assembled. They voted to hear the vice-chancellor's speech. The vice-chancellor was later to assert that there was a hard core of about 50 students who were determined to disturb the institution. Sheffield University was in fact in the process of finding methods of involving students in university affairs. So, too, were Keele and Essex. At Leeds a working party was set up to perform a similar function. In the belief that student participation would blunt the edge of revolt some vice-chancellors hastened to give their students responsibility. In accordance with the agreement with the N.U.S. they treated their students as adults in the expectation that they would behave like adults. It should be remembered that the vote was about to be given to all those over 18.

Meanwhile the Pakistani revolutionary was touring the North in search of support for the October 27 Demonstration. He spoke at Oxford, Nottingham and other places to large crowds. Little October 27 committees sprang up in many universities and coaches were ordered for the day. Some universities, it is true, seemed less concerned about world politics than others. At Manchester, for instance, of 11,000 university students only 29 appeared for a march on behalf of Mexican progressives.

In London itself unease grew. In the second week of October there was an attempt at arson at the Imperial War Museum. Firms on the projected line of march took due precautions. It was arranged that three principal art museums should be kept safely closed.

On October 15 there was a small demonstration in support of Dr. Benjamin Spock's opposition to the Vietnam War. Miss Vanessa Redgrave was prominent in this. There was a demonstration of 20 students at Regent Street Polytechnic. They alleged that some of the governors had a financial interest in racialism.

On the 17th Mr. Peter Ustinov took office as rector of Dundee University. He made a speech in which he asserted that militancy in all its forms was the surrender of the weak majority to the strong minority. He said that there was a solemn duty to ensure that there would never be a risk that the shy thought, shyly expressed by the shy man, would be shouted down 'for that thought might well be the most valuable of the lot'. In a later sit-in a bust of Mr. Ustinov was covered in a red sheet.

Meanwhile the L.S.E. was preparing for the 27th. At a students' union meeting a resolution to occupy the institution to provide accommodation and sanctuary for the marchers was carried. It had been voted to the top of the agenda. 321 people voted for occupation and 208 against it. 32 abstained. As soon as the resolution was carried the meeting became inquorate—the L.S.E. quorum was then 60—and the governors' offer of more representation was not discussed, let alone accepted.

There was immediate opposition to the prospect of occupation and a petition was launched for the calling of another union meeting to reverse the previous decision. A committee of eight was elected. Four were Conservatives, two Labour Club members and two Liberals. A thousand signatures were collected.

Another meeting, the largest ever held up to then, was convened. Mr. Colin Crouch, the president of the union and ex-president of the Labour Club, spoke for reversal. After two and a half hours the vote was for reversal. The Socialist Society insisted on a recount. The gap narrowed to 598 to 592 votes. After an hour and a half of procedural wrangles of this sort a motion declaring the union neutral was passed 'by acclamation'. L.S.E. lurched confusedly into occupation. Most of those who had voted for occupation did not in fact stay to a further meeting that night. Of those who remained a majority of 186 decided that the occupation should begin immediately. L.S.E. was ready for the October 27 weekend.

During the struggle for L.S.E. the government had been taking precautions. A well-known French revolutionary student was denied admission to the country to campaign for the rectorship of Glasgow University. This election was won by a former moderator of the Church of Scotland—who obtained an overwhelming majority. Police reinforcements were called in. There were attempts to play down rumours that such institutions as the House of Commons and the gentlemen's lavatory in Piccadilly Circus would be damaged on the 27th. Scare stories were, on the whole, discounted.

L.S.E. Extreme Left might well have envied the solidarity of Birmingham College of Education where the students were claiming 99 per solidarity for a boycott of lectures in their attempt to compel their authorities to provide better bus services between the main buildings and the annexe. Hatfield College of Technology announced that by reasonable negotiations it had been agreed that students should sit on the governing board. It should not be forgotten that events at L.S.E. and similar institutions were not necessarily representative of tendencies and interests at the majority of colleges.

October 27 came closer. The possibility of violence divided the movement. The South-East Young Liberals' executive voted thirteen to four against supporting the March. By a large majority the students' union of King's College, London, condemned 'the trend towards violence in student demonstrations and activities'. Swansea students' union announced that the possibility of violence had reduced the numbers of its students who would go. Mr. Geoffrey Martin of the N.U.S. executive warned the 400,000 students of Britain not to go on the March. This warning was immediately condemned by Sussex, Essex and Kent universities and ignored by most of the others. The N.U.S. branch of the North-Western region disagreed with Mr. Martin's statement and asserted that he had no right to make it.

At Colchester 40 Essex University students were arrested for obstructing traffic in the rush hour during a demonstration to bring attention to the Vietnam March. The police were assisted by the obstructed citizens. The students' union representative council at once condemned the arrests, planned to set up a legal aid fund and asked the Home Secretary for an enquiry.

A Conservative M.P. described the leaders of the marchers as 'foreign scum' and demanded stern measures. He had 61 supporters in the House of Commons.

Some universities pursued their private interests. An agreement was reached at York to the effect that four of the 40 members of the General Academic Board were to be students. At Oxford there was a demonstration by about 100 of the Oxford Revolutionary Socialist Students against the wearing of gowns and the whole process of matriculation. Surrey University was in the throes of moving en bloc from one site to another.

The days immediately before the March were extremely confused. Far from its being a long-planned plot it was uncertain until almost the last moment in what order they should march. Many of the organizations involved feared that the Maoists would enter Grosvenor Square and provoke a battle with the police. In order to avoid being placed in the difficult moral position of either condemning or condoning any such violence the marchers decided in heated discussions at the L.S.E. that the Maoists should be contained by the more orthodox communists.

It is hardly surprising that unity of purpose was so difficult to obtain. Those groups involved included the Communists, the Young Liberals, the Young Socialists, the Independent Labour Party, the London Mayday Manifesto Committee, the International Socialists, the Lords of Anarchy and the advocates of Victory to the Engineers. There were innumerable others.

The L.S.E. had by now been closed by its director Dr. Walter Adams. This had not been effective and many hitherto non-involved students joined the occupation temporarily. Some of the staff supported the occupation. One alleged that he was prepared to risk losing his job. He still teaches there.

University College, London, students' union condemned violence by a large majority though a proposal that the use of its

facilities should be offered to the police was defeated. Other
London colleges showed the same unwillingness to involve themselves officially in the planned demonstration.

The March took place. It proved something of an anti-climax.
About 25,000 people marched. This was half the hoped-for number. The only acts of violence that occurred were committed by
the Maoists in Grosvenor Square. They had succeeded in getting
out of the position insisted on by their very temporary allies. Led
by an L.S.E. lecturer, among others, they reached Grosvenor
Square and a battle with the police took place. In the course of this
a policeman was held by one marcher while another kicked him
on the head.

The March had no effect on the Vietnam war. 13 per cent of
those marching, according to a survey published in *New Society*,
did not know that peace talks were going on in Paris. The
marchers were divided in their hopes for peace. 52 per cent hoped
for a Vietcong victory and 42 per cent hoped for a compromise
peace. 6 per cent did not know what they wanted. Only just over
half were students. Of these 28 per cent were sociology students.
10 per cent were, or had been at some time, anarchists. 70 per cent
had expected there to be violence on the March. The extent of the
marchers' commitment to the issue of Vietnam can be gauged from
the support given to a demonstration about the South-East Asian
War a year later. 300 people attended.

Any expectations that the structure of Western capitalism would
be undermined were disappointed. On December 3, 1968 the
Dow-Jones Index reached its highest point up to that date.

There was one result which should be mentioned. The War On
Want campaign suffered from a sudden withdrawal of support for
the rumour had been spread that this organization had been
feeding the students occupying L.S.E.

This ended the first stage of the student disturbances of 1968–9.
The academic year had started with a massive, successful and
unpunished occupation of a university institution. The Campus
Reform Campaign of the N.U.S. had disappeared.

The implications of these events were widely and quickly
grasped. There was, on October 30, a small sit-in, the second in
two weeks, at Birmingham University. About 100 students sat
down for representation on the Senate. At Manchester College

of Commerce 200 students voted, on the same day, for action against the inadequacy of the library facilities. On November 4 70 of the students were in occupation. This episode, indeed, illustrates more clearly than most the problems of expansion and finance. For the 2,000 students in the college there were only 166 library seats and 15,000 books. Moreover the library was not open all day. Two councillors came in to talk to the occupiers and pointed out that half the money received from the government by the city was spent on education and slum-clearance. Priority was given to primary schools. The council refused to negotiate officially until the sit-in stopped. The chief education officer proposed that the establishments committee should provide two more library staff. Eventually these were provided on a temporary basis and the library was kept open from nine in the morning to nine at night. These utilitarian demands contrasted with those of the Socialist Society at the University of Manchester Institute of Science and Technology. Here there were complaints of overwork and under-representation. There were, however, staff-student committees in every department and students had representation on sixteen Institute committees.

Oxford had its troubles. The Oxford Revolutionary Socialist Students conducted a campaign against All Souls' which they regarded as the citadel of privilege. It was defended—in a physical sense sometimes—by Warden Sparrow's supporters. On November 5 100 of these students attempted to force their way into a meeting of Congregation, one of the bodies responsible for running the University.

Meanwhile at the centre of unrest October 27 provided further occasion for strife. At L.S.E. Lord Robbins on behalf of the court of governors warned that although this time those staff involved in the occupation would, in view of their immaturity, not be punished they might be treated with less indulgence in future. The Professor of English Law protested against this threat to academic freedom and was supported by 40 of his colleagues. On November 1 a students' union meeting condemned by 229 votes to 85 both the court of governors and the president of the union. Mr. Crouch resigned and so did the rest of the students' representative council. New elections were held and the Socialist Society candidates were defeated, in most cases by about 200 votes. Political feeling in the institution was still intense and the poll was one of the highest recorded—about 1,400.

Many institutions remained conservative in student activities. At Bournemouth College of Technology 1,000 staff and students voted against the government's decision not to build a new college, merged from several, on a large new site. 200 of these began an occupation—but these demonstrations were stopped for Armistice Day. At Edinburgh University Mr. Kenneth Allsop was by a large majority elected rector, defeating the two student candidates. At Leeds the only student activity to attract much notice was the kidnapping of Miss Anita Harris as a rag stunt. Rags, indeed, provided publicity for other institutions. Four students from Enfield College of Technology climbed over the walls of Buckingham Palace. Guildford students tried to steal pieces of London Bridge.

On November 10 the Revolutionary Socialist Students' Federation held a conference at the Round House, North London. Of its 2,500 members 400 attended. They compiled a programme of action. Their plans included the supersession of students' unions' bureaucracy by 'instant democracy', the offer of higher education to all who wanted it, the abolition of examinations, the administration of institutions by general assemblies of staff, students and workers, the suppression of bourgeois ideological content in lectures and courses, the heckling of lecturers and the invasion of meetings of boards of governors. To this end examination boycotts were considered for Oxford, Manchester, Hull and Essex. The R.S.S.F. had now completely replaced the R.S.A. This had never claimed more than 800 adherents. Essex, L.S.E. and Oxford were reported to have the largest branches of the R.S.S.F. They claimed between 200 and 300 members each. It is worth remembering that there were 400,000 students in Britain.

The only sit-in to attract much public attention between October 27 and November 29 was a small and brief though well-publicized one at the Inns of Court. This took place on November 12 and 13. It involved only 40 students at any one time although it had been voted for by 257 to 10. The reason for the sit-in was that the Council for Legal Education had introduced a new regulation forbidding students more than four attempts at passing their examinations. Previously some students had been taking these

examinations twenty times. Most of those involved were foreign
students from underdeveloped countries. The only other 'direct
protest' involving a majority of foreign students occurred at a hall
of residence at Woolwich Polytechnic. Here there was a dispute
about heating arrangements and 40 of the 70 students formed
themselves into a committee to resist the expulsion of one student
over this dispute. These were the only two institutions in which the
majority of those involved in a disturbance were foreign.

On November 16 there was a spontaneous sit-in at Hendon
College of Technology. Here the cause was immediate and local
indeed. Students had found that their evening meal was un-
available as the mayor of Barnet and others were to be enter-
tained.

Student representation continued to be an issue. On November
23 the City University, London, demanded one-third representation on the Senate.

Partly as a result of all these manifestations of dissatisfaction the
House of Commons decided to set up a select committee of enquiry
into student unrest and higher education.

Hardly had the House of Commons come to this decision when
the N.U.S. had its autumn conference, where much of the government's policy was attacked. One student, Mr. Peter Cadogan from
Swansea, proposed that in view of the country's economic situation
the N.U.S. should not press for priority for an increase in grants
for students. This proposal was defeated. The N.U.S. demanded
automatic re-sits for students failing examinations. A proposal to
make the N.U.S. vulnerable to political use failed narrowly on a
card vote. To pass, it would have needed a two-thirds majority.
It would not be unfair to suggest that the sole achievement of this
conference was to drink the main conference hotel dry. Mr.
Martin, of the N.U.S. executive, described the conference as
something of a farce. He continued to draft the agreement on
colleges that he was hoping to sign with the County Councils
Association, the Association of Municipal Corporations, the
Association of Education Committees, the Inner London Education
Authority and the Welsh Joint Education Committee. The object
of this agreement was to ensure that students at colleges of further
education were given representation on governing bodies. Since
over 300 of the 900 involved had no student unions his task was

difficult. Both the conference and the negotiations showed clearly that students were not a homogeneous body with a coherent policy and a representative executive.

It was clear already that the events of October had encouraged a belief that disturbances would go unpunished. Students plucked up courage and sat down. However, in the lull after October these disturbances had been scattered and on a small scale.

The second stage of revolt consisted of the realization by the students of both Birmingham and Bristol that they could do what L.S.E. students had done. In both cases there was little obvious cause for unrest.

The Birmingham sit-in started almost as the N.U.S. finished its deliberations at Margate. The issue was student representation on the University senate and its committees. In May a staff-student working party had produced a document called 'Student Role'. This had recommended student representation. However, without infringing the University Charter the senate could not grant votes to the students who were to represent their colleagues on the committees. On November 27, of the 6,000 Birmingham students, 200 students sat-in in protest. On November 20 300 had attended a campus reform emergency meeting and the last week in November had been set as the deadline for the senate to concede to the demands for representation. The day after the sit-in began it was made official by the guild. 1,000 students attended this meeting on November 28. The following day they voted, in about the same numbers, to continue the sit-in indefinitely or until their demands were met. The first days of the sit-in were distinguished by the breaking open of the filing cabinets in the vice-chancellor's office and the photostating of various confidential documents. For a brief space, indeed, the vice-chancellor was imprisoned in his office by a few dozen of the occupiers. At one point the internal telephone exchange was occupied.

On December 2 a meeting of over 2,000 decided to continue the occupation. It demanded that no one should be victimized, that a 50 per cent student university commission should be set up to consider the running of the university, that committee meetings should be opened except when they dealt with personal matters and that the principle of student participation should be accepted.

The vice-chancellor, Dr. Brockie Hunter, asserted that there

2

would be no negotiations until the occupation stopped and that no one should be punished for free expression of opinion.

On December 3 a meeting of over 4,000 students voted 2,346 to 1,542 to end the occupation. After a meeting of five and a half hours the Guild Executive voted 71 to 42 to ignore this decision. On December 4 the vice-chancellor gave permission for a Guild meeting to be held in the Great Hall and extended until five o'clock to discuss the matter. 2,000 attended and the meeting voted for opposition to discipline. The meeting ended at 7.10. It had lasted over four hours. Those who left afterwards signed statements that they had been in the Hall after the time-limit expired.

The University decided that the Degree Convocation would be held not on the premises but in the Town Hall.

On December 5 a statement from the vice-chancellor was read out to a student gathering. It confirmed explicitly that no one would be punished for taking part in the sit-in and left unclear what the University intended to do about those who had actually broken the law. By about 2,000 votes to 12, according to a *Times* reporter, or by about 4,000 votes to 30 according to the guild secretary (an ardent organizer of the occupation), the students present voted to end the occupation. It should be made clear that most of those who were involved were only technically occupiers and in fact went home at night.

Thus the second large-scale sit-in of the year ended unpunished. It is hardly surprising that another broke out immediately. This one took place at Bristol University. Here negotiations had been going on for some time about the possibility of opening the students' union facilities to the students of the other colleges in the area. Two years before the students' union had voted down such a proposal but it had changed its views and was pressing for such reciprocal membership. This would have infringed the union constitution. So before embarking on the complex proceedings necessary for a change in the union constitution the vice-chancellor, Sir Roderick Collar, was planning to set up a working party of staff, student representatives and members of the local colleges to examine the whole matter. This satisfied most of the students, of which there were 3,000 at the University, but 300 began to sit in. Unlike the Birmingham sit-in this attracted virtually no further active support. The vice-chancellor cut off the heating and issued writs against eight ringleaders. A union meeting voted 773 to 215, 87 abstaining, to end the sit-in. This decision was ignored by the occupiers. On December 15 the sit-in ended. Attrition did what frontal onslaught could not.

It must not be assumed that these were the only two disturbances of this period. 30 Sheffield students demonstrated for choice of lodgings. On the day the Birmingham sit-in began Salford students protested to Prince Philip, then visiting them in his capacity as chancellor, a post which the students had just voted to keep, about the inadequacy of library facilities. There were 150 library seats for 3,000 students. Similarly tangible dissatisfactions moved an unusually large proportion of any student body to action at Kingston College of Technology where 1,800 students boycotted the refectory in protest against alleged bad food. At Loughborough the president of the union was debagged.

More distant issues disturbed less utilitarian institutions. On December 5 Professor Trevor-Roper had come to give a history lecture for L.S.E. Oration Day. By threatening to disrupt this lecture, L.S.E. Socialist Society compelled Professor Trevor-Roper to be the target of a 'discussion' on Greece. On December 10 150 Essex students declared a two-day strike on behalf of Biafra and picketed one or two university buildings. On December 12 about 30 of them together with about the same number from East Anglia University occupied a room in the House of Commons and were removed by the police.

Some institutions tried to avert trouble. At Sussex, it was announced on December 4, seven students were to sit on the senate. At Oriel College, Oxford, students were given, on December 10, the right to sit on various bodies, including the rules committee. Perhaps the attitude of one Leeds professor was more realistic; he burnt all his confidential personal files on students.

There were a few minor scares. Corresponding to the Great Red Plot theory there has long been a counter-theory—the Great Establishment Conspiracy. Allegations were made at Sussex and Nottingham universities that police were trying to extract information from students about their colleagues. The Ministry of Defence was dragged in.

The year 1968 ended academically not with a student revolt but with financial wrangles and inconsistencies. The local education authorities refused to support the Open University. The government announced a decrease in the estimates for further education and 150 places at Manchester colleges 'disappeared'. At the same time it was discovered that twice as many people were taking A-levels as in 1960. However, by far the greatest feeling was aroused by the suggestion, late in December, of the Prices and Incomes Board that on the new salary scale university lecturers should be assessed partly as teachers and that this assessment should be influenced by the views of their students. This was in fact only part of a complicated and not ungenerous set of arrangements, but the Prices and Income Board did not realize that the transmission of wisdom could hardly be computed by anyone—least of all its recipients. There was a storm of protest. The vice-chancellor of Liverpool University resigned. The public protested. The Association of University Teachers threatened industrial action if the acquisition of knowledge were treated as an industry. The only organizations to approve were the N.U.S. and the R.S.A.—the latter was almost defunct and the former had no influence. The Prime Minister, who had been a don, dismissed the P.I.B.'s suggestion. However, bitter feelings had been aroused and some university teachers began to fear not only excessive expansion and student unrest but state intervention in academic matters.

Thus the second stage of student disturbances in the academic year 1968–9 ended. The example of L.S.E. had been followed. The unpunished activities of the sit-in had been extended to include theft and the deliberate prevention of the administration of universities. The principle was firmly established that violence would not be considered necessary cause for expulsion. It is an ironic commentary on these attempts to 'politicize' the universities that the results of lowering the voting age to 18 showed that the young as a whole were alarmingly apathetic. Even appeals on T.V. and in the Press from all three parties could not persuade all the young to register on the electoral rolls. Only about 65 per cent did so—and the figure was not much higher among students despite the pleas of the N.U.S.

The third stage of the year's student unrest was more protracted and violent. Public attention concentrated on the original centre of disturbance, the London School of Economics. Forecasts made in the Christmas vacation that the School would soon be closed were justified by events. The general expectation of trouble and the general anxiety over university finance were such that the proposed establishment of an independent university was greeted with fervour in many quarters. Of its organizers one was Professor Ferns of Birmingham University and another was Sir Sidney Caine, former director of the L.S.E. Financial restrictions on universities were such that Coventry council was advised to cut its annual grant of £20,000 to Warwick University, to £5,000. The year 1969 started, in fact, with an intensification of the pressures of the previous year.

L.S.E. authorities opened the term with the granting of an honorary fellowship to M. Trudeau, the Prime Minister of Canada. Possibly this was an attempt to be in step with the times. If so, it left the Extreme Left-wing students unimpressed. A week-long teach-in was held on Rhodesia with the willing co-operation of the School authorities. This proved disastrous. On January 10 Dr. Walter Adams was shouted down when he addressed an audience of 500 students. Some of them alleged that L.S.E. investments were buttressing Rhodesian and South African racialism. At a very much smaller meeting later the same day it was decided to prevent the governors 'by force if necessary' from using the facilities of the School and to stop certain large corporations with interests in Rhodesia and South Africa from recruiting staff on L.S.E. premises. Some students, a smaller number still, decided to sit down in front of Dr. Adams' office until he came out and discussed their demands. As he was out they were compelled to occupy the senior common-room instead. At the teach-in itself in the evening, further excitement was caused by the appearance of a few dozen of the National Front. These shouted down one of the speakers, who was so upset that he fainted at the microphone. This led to scuffles.

This issue continued to disturb L.S.E. On January 12 there was a 400-strong 'march of dignity' on Rhodesia House and South Africa House. This became a pitched battle. The marchers included Black Power supporters, Young Communists and members of the Liberal and Labour parties. The police separated them and about 150 of the National Front.

So far the other educational institutions of Britain had been relatively quiet. At Glasgow, however, about 100 students walked out of the opening lecture of a series on military defence. At Essex about 50 students sat-in in the computer department because of the expulsion of a student. This sit-in was brief. There was, however, at this time a lot of trouble about the visits of Right-wing M.P.s to, or near, various colleges.

Meanwhile, meeting succeeded meeting at L.S.E. Such meetings became smaller. Further occasion for student indignation was provided by the mention of the possible use of force by staff in a report by the general purposes committee. This also reminded staff that they could be sacked for 'incapacity' or 'misconduct'. A fresh source of trouble was discovered in the L.S.E. gates. These internal gates had been planned since the summer of 1968. It was alleged by the authorities, when their existence was noticed, that they were erected to check domestic thefts. In view of the losses by theft of library books alone this was quite credible. The gates which could cut off sections of L.S.E. from one another had been there for several weeks before being noticed and being made the subject of complaint. Thus agitation was intensified.

There was still little disturbance at other colleges. The students' union of Regent Street Polytechnic voted against forcibly excluding the representatives of firms with interests in South Africa and Rhodesia. A demonstration against such firms attracted only about 20 supporters. The previous term the Commons select committee investigating higher education had been told at Regent Street that the student image had become such that lodgings were now harder to obtain than ever. At Manchester the boycott of examinations planned by the R.S.S.F. proved to have little appeal. 25 students boycotted a history examination. At Aberystwyth University College 60 students sat-in in protest against the political use being made of the University of Wales by the proposed dispatch there of Prince Charles.

In the week ending January 25 matters reached a climax in L.S.E. and student disturbances once more achieved the invidious distinction of headlines in all the national newspapers. There was an unprecedented number of meetings in this week. Attempts were made to calm tempers. On January 22 a meeting of the staff academic board dropped the general purposes committee's mention of the possible use of force. The 9 student representatives present objected to a clause recommending that students recognize the obligation to identify those guilty of disrupting lectures.

Southern Africa forgotten, the attack now concentrated on the gates. At first the opponents of destruction held their own or, to be more accurate, sat through the meetings at which the Extreme Left brought in proposals for the immediate demolition of the gates. On January 23 the students' union carried a proposal, by 363 to 332 votes, maintaining the principle that the gates should be removed but noting the legal consequences of doing so. The Extreme Left set a dead-line. If the gates were not, by the next day, scheduled for removal they would be removed anyway. The next day, at the fourth meeting of the week, the proposal for the immediate demolition of the gates was carried by 282 to about 240. The gates were duly demolished with the instruments brought by the Extreme Left to the meeting to discuss the proposal. The authorities of L.S.E. closed the School and invoked the aid of the police. There was a minor riot and 30 students were taken to Bow Street. There was then a sit-down outside Bow Street.

Deprived of L.S.E. the Extreme Left marched on the University of London Union. There the keys of the officials running the union building were forcibly removed and the Extreme Left settled into occupation. This was done by 250 students after 750 had marched on L.S.E. only to find it defended by the police. During this sit-in the canteen was robbed.

A meeting of 500 was held at the Union on January 27. Proposals for the dismissal of staff who had identified students to the police and that such staff should be brought before staff-student tribunals were voted down.

On January 28 there were fewer in the Union. Of the L.S.E. students present 97 voted to end the occupation and 7 advocated its continuance. When all present voted, the proposal for ending the sit-in was carried by 226 to 120. On the same day a meeting of 200 of those opposed to disruption passed a resolution both dissociating themselves from violence and opposing the re-erection of the gates. The problem of the U.L.U. occupation was solved later in the day by medical students who compelled L.S.E. Extreme Left and its supporters to leave.

Meanwhile L.S.E. authorities had not been idle. On January 28 the academic board condemned the previous Friday's violence by 'a group of students and outsiders against school property'. Dr.

Adams made it clear that the re-erection of the gates was not a pre-condition of the reopening of the School. Legal proceedings were being set on foot against those who had actually destroyed the gates.

These disturbances provided an occasion for disturbances and attempted disturbances in other institutions. 200 Warwick students met unofficially and occupied the library in support of L.S.E. students' resistance to gates. At the largest official union meeting held to that date they obtained official union blessing for the occupation. They also organized a march through the town to explain the issue to the townsfolk. The only previous issue to attract such widespread student attention had been raised in December 1968 when the story of Winnie-the-Pooh had been inscribed by an unknown hand on some of the university paving-stones. The attempt of the authorities to remove these inscriptions had been viewed as oppression.

On January 29 150 students of the London School for Oriental and African Studies registered their support of L.S.E. students. The Borough Polytechnic students' union gave support for L.S.E. students' struggle for academic freedom. 100 Cambridge students began a 24-hour sympathy sit-in. 500 Essex students occupied the lecture theatre block and began a 24-hour sit-in. It was not a happy day for the Minister of Education to announce that an extra £50 million would be spent on the universities in the years 1970–1972.

The following day 13 people accused of actually destroying the gates were banned by legal injunction from entering L.S.E. or taking part in its affairs. 10 of these were registered L.S.E. students. The Left had hoped for several thousand students to support action against this. About 400 students met at U.L.U. The meeting condemned the injunctions and with many more students marched to L.S.E. and down Fleet Street. The L.S.E. was guarded by 150 police. Outside the offices of the *Financial Times* several copies of this paper were set on fire; Lord Robbins is not only chairman of L.S.E. governors but on the board of the *Financial Times*. During their absence from U.L.U. 200 opponents of disruption garrisoned it and prevented the Extreme Left's re-entry for another occupation.

On the same day 400 of the Essex occupiers voted to continue their sit-in until the L.S.E. was reopened. 150 of the O.R.S.S. voted for 'a day of action' in support of L.S.E. students.

Solidarity was less successful elsewhere. At Sussex a union meeting sympathetic to L.S.E. students voted overwhelmingly not to occupy the administration block; the vice-chancellor had stated that he was prepared to act firmly. Attempts at a sit-in at Southampton on behalf of the banned 13 failed; a meeting of 1,400 expressed sympathy—and decided not to occupy. The four dozen who ignored this decision were themselves ignored. 200 Cambridge students who voted to remove their gates were prevented from doing so by several hundred others who assembled outside Cambridge Senate House. An attempt to organize a sit-in at Hull was unsuccessful. At Kent an ill-supported sit-in lasted 18 hours. It was condemned by the students' union. Its call for a mass meeting was almost totally ignored. At Swansea University College a meeting of 1,200 students deplored 'the recent actions of a minority of students from L.S.E.' Perhaps the most typical reaction was at Imperial College, London. There a meeting voted, by 579 to 50 with 41 abstentions, in favour of 'militant apathy'. Perhaps the smallest demonstration was at East Anglia University where 30 students held a picket of the arts block to protest at 'the increasingly repressive attitude of authorities to both students and workers'.

It must not be supposed that the L.S.E. gates were the only occasion for trouble during the closure. At Bristol University the president of the union, who had recently accepted an invitation to explain to some U.S. notables what made British students tick, resigned his office on the grounds that the Extreme Left was making his task impossible by throwing the whole student body into confusion. Bristol authorities had withdrawn the writs against eight leaders of the sit-in and were trying to wear the disrupters down.

Meanwhile these disturbances had been punctuated by a great meeting of L.S.E. students held on February 3 at the Friends' House, Euston. Between 1,700 and 2,000 students attended in the hope that their collective wisdom would solve the School's problems or at least enable the place to be reopened. Various proposals were put to the meeting and some carried. The meeting decided that the demolition of the gates had been justified but that such methods were to be avoided for the future, that the 13 victimized people should be protected by the union but that the meeting should not go on a march of solidarity as soon as the proceedings ended. It decided in favour of more participation in college affairs and in favour of fewer meetings. It voted against the principle of violence and for the election of 22 of those who had supported violence to a special *ad hoc* committee of 23. It should be said that, at this time, the students' union was technically leaderless as the president and council had resigned for fear of the legal consequences of the destruction of the gates. After the meeting 2,000 people, most of whom were not from L.S.E., marched to Houghton Street. The L.S.E. was protected by police; some were mounted.

The same day Balliol College undergraduates voted to show solidarity with L.S.E. students and to spend £25 on explaining to their fellow-students and the townsfolk what the issues were. They must have had great confidence in their powers of perception.

In the circumstances Dr. Adams delayed reopening the School. However, there was great pressure on him. The advice from both the R.S.S.F. and the N.U.S. could be safely ignored. That from the staff could not. On February 6 the academic board passed a resolution for the School to be reopened the following week. A proposal for an enquiry into the School's affairs and the suspension of disciplinary proceedings till then was put by Professor Mackenzie and carried by the meeting. By 69 votes to 33 the academic board approved a resolution calling for the reopening of the School and promising 'full and active co-operation with any measures taken by the director to maintain good order'.

On February 11 it was announced that the L.S.E. would reopen the following week. The announcement made it clear that further disruption might lead to further closures and that these might affect student grants. On behalf of the committee of 23 a statement was issued in response. It ran: 'Only trouble can come from these proposals. Lord Robbins has held the views of the staff and students in contempt and has spurned our conciliatory gestures. By re-opening the School on these terms he is running the risk of L.S.E. being closed down permanently.'

The week before the reopening was not entirely without incident in the politics of youth. The Young Conservatives' conference in Bournemouth passed, by a narrow majority, a proposal recom-

mending the reinstatement of Mr. Powell in the shadow cabinet.
Mr. Heath ignored this advice. A Leeds student returned his gold
medal to the Duke of Edinburgh on the grounds that the Duke
had said that students with gold medals were unlikely to protest.
The student had been involved in a protest. At Essex there was a
three-day Festival of Revolution with appropriate slogans on walls.

On February 18 L.S.E. was reopened. The Extreme Left held a
Carnival of Reopening. The authorities allowed the ten banned
students in to work but forbade them to take part in students'
union affairs. L.S.E.'s reopening coincided with a drugs case con-
cerning Essex University.

On February 19 a meeting of the students' union was held at
L.S.E. Over 1,000 students attended. Again they promised solidarity in the face of discipline for some and again they voted
against immediate action. 686 voted against an occupation and
380 voted for it. The meeting voted four to one in favour of an
independent enquiry and two to one in favour of non-violence.
The chairman of the Conservative Association, Mr. Richard
Osband, proposed that the student body should support 'the course
of natural justice'. This was voted down by three to one for the
disrupters. It was, however, now apparent that most students
would make little effort for their erring brethren. Two days later
the injunctions forbidding the banned ten to take part in School
politics were extended. They had been ignored.

On the same day the Duke of Edinburgh gave his views on some
forms of student protest:

> . . . it is a mob activity. There is no individuality about it. The
> argument is a chanted argument. There is no reason in it. . . .
> How is it that they lose all this impetus the moment they leave
> university? This seems to me to be the criterion, that people
> should continue to have fire in their bellies, should continue to
> want to change things, in a legitimate and sensible way . . . a
> lot of people without perhaps sufficient experience found them-
> selves in positions of responsibility and authority.

The Duke had little cause for personal concern. His son's extra-
curricular university activities were confined to acting in a revue.
The Cambridge branch of the R.S.S.F. started during the L.S.E.
closure did not include Prince Charles.

Excitement subsided for the time being. Even the announcement that university numbers had passed the Robbins mark
aroused little feeling—for the moment. There was a temporary
revival of the Great Establishment Conspiracy theory when a
Keele student told the Commons select committee enquiring into
higher education that Special Branch men had been attending
student meetings, photographing students and preparing secret
documents on some students after a recent sit-in.

However at the centre of disturbance a sense of unease was
maintained. The three student seats on L.S.E. general purposes
committee were on February 25 filled by election. The poll was
low and three victors, all banned by injunction, received respectively 422, 396 and 354 votes. The following day the academic
board met and welcomed student acceptance of greater participation in running the School. The board passed, by 120 votes to 8, a
resolution that the School should remain open unless there was no
reasonable prospect of its being able to continue to fulfil its
academic functions. Dr. Adams had promised the board that there
would be no announcements of further extended closures without
prior consultation. This prevented Professor Mackenzie from
bringing forward a proposal to this effect.

On February 28 the students' union rejected a proposed occupation by 415 votes to 380. Meetings were now shrinking.

Other institutions were also somewhat quieter. The City University was about to follow the example of Bradford University
which on February 5 had given students representation on a senate
decision-making body. At Bradford 9 of the 45 members of the
general purposes committee were students. Now the City University was to have 6 students attending a senate meeting
and 75 students on committees. At Oxford, where on February 6
200 of the O.R.S.S. had voted in condemnation of the Education
Minister's attack on 'the thugs of the academic world', the O.R.S.S.
candidate was on March 7 defeated for the presidency of the Union
—by a communist.

On March 7 there was a hunger-strike at Aberystwyth University
College because of 'the political use being made of the college by
the government in sending Prince Charles here to be a student
next term'. On March 10 40 Bangor students sat-in for the same
reason. On the same day L.S.E. Extreme Left obtained union

sanction by 355 votes to 206 for an occupation on behalf of colleagues threatened with discipline. This was marked by the breaking-open of the files in the room of the Dean of Undergraduates and the circularization of the minutes of staff and governors' meetings. This break-in necessitated the resetting of some examination papers. The occupation was unnoticed, except for slogans painted on the walls, by most students and was rescinded two days later at a smaller meeting. On March 15 a union meeting elected a new honorary life member. Lord Robbins was defeated for this honour. On this note term ended.

At Essex students had occupied the administration block in sympathy with L.S.E. This occupation, too, was short-lived. Meanwhile pressure was being applied at Bristol. Two of those involved in the December occupation were offered the choice of immediate signature of a good behaviour contract or immediate expulsion. The imminence of the summer examinations made mass action on their behalf unlikely.

More important facts went unnoticed. There was a drop of a fifth in the number of overseas students. This was a direct result of the raising of fees for overseas students. Oxford and Bradford resisted this with great vigour. There was also an alarming shortfall in candidates taking up university places in science, technology and medicine. Shortly afterwards new places were created in these subjects.

During the university vacation the N.U.S. held its spring conference. It pressed for the increase of grants to the full level recommended the previous year by an advisory panel under a Leeds professor. To the surprise of many, Mr. Trevor Fisk, the president of the N.U.S., was voted out by 273 votes to 181 and replaced by Mr. Jack Straw. The victor commented, 'I stood on the platform for making the N.U.S. more active and in trying to transform it into a real student movement. I think I have received a mandate to do that.' He wanted the N.U.S. to work closely with individual colleges. He thought that the N.U.S. should support students in college disputes, if three conditions were fulfilled. The student's case should be in line with N.U.S. policy; it should be non-violent; and it should have the support of most students in the college. Mr. Straw was fortunate in finding one such case in his year of office. He began a policy of recruiting sixth-formers.

The N.U.S. rescinded the previous year's agreement with the Association of Education Committees on student representation. Henceforth bargaining was to take place at local levels. Mr. Straw believed that academic disputes resembled industrial ones. The representatives of those institutions most affected carried a proposal condemning 'the use of legal action by a university or college authority for any academic issue'. There was overwhelming support for a resolution for a National Day of Student Action on May 28 for art college students. None of these decisions influenced anyone.

Meanwhile at local level matters continued much as before. There was a well-supported boycott at Leicester College of Education because of an alleged case of drug-addiction. When the police had been called in it was discovered that the syringe, the discovery of which caused the trouble, had almost certainly been used by a diabetic to inject insulin. Edinburgh students took over an empty house to lodge squatters. Sir Douglas Logan, Principal of London University, told the Commons select committee that after discussions with properly elected student representatives he was subjected to minority pressures. He cited the case of the London University Lodgings bureau case. A small revolutionary group had passed a motion condemning 'racialist actions'. The resulting demonstration had closed the bureau. On the same day as Sir Douglas's complaint police were called to Enfield College of Technology where arts students were trying to disrupt a careers conference intended for science students only. The occasion for complaint was that the conference was being attended by army, navy and air force officers.

At Southampton University the term had ended with the election of a well-known train-robber to honorary life-membership of the union. The vote had been 128 to 121. The president of the union explained: 'This is a protest against the sentence which was passed on Mr. ——. Most murderers get less than 25 years and the only conclusion we can draw is that the law is more concerned to protect property than life.'

The comparative quiet enabled the Labour and Conservative students to stir to life. Mr. Hugh Anderson of Cambridge, later to found the Students for Labour Victory movement, complained on March 31 that British universities should not be having sporting and cultural contacts with South Africa. This was a foretaste of future disturbances. On the same day the Federation of Conservative Students elected its officers for the year. The new chairman was Mr. Stephen Kreppel of L.S.E. The vice-presidents were Mr. Francis Dobbyn of L.S.E., Mr. Howard Flight of Magdalene College, Cambridge, and Mr. Peter Martin of St. Andrews. Mr. Kreppel was one of the advocates of 'the course of natural justice for disrupters'. Youthful Liberals were not to be out-publicized. 28 of them, the following day, held a sit-down in Trafalgar Square Post Office where they burnt an envelope addressed to the Prime Minister. The point of this act was that the envelope bore a stamp commemorating the foundation of N.A.T.O. Sit-ins indeed occurred in unexpected places. On April 1 a student was fined for leading a sit-in in a vicarage.

During this lull the Black Paper was published. This was an attack by various dons and teachers on 'progressive' theory and practice. Streaming and selection in schools were defended. Student power was attacked—and student participation hardly taken seriously. The publication of this book immediately divided the educational world more definitely than it had ever been divided before. Its publication coincided with the forecast that student numbers might double by 1982. The only crumb of comfort in the vacation for the educational traditionalists was that applicants for sociology places at university had dropped by 37 per cent over the past year.

Some universities were, of course, continuing along the paths of negotiation. Manchester University senate agreed on April 1 to set up a committee of equal numbers of staff and students as part of a three-year experiment to improve staff-student relations and bring about substantial student representation. Some university students were in trouble for quite different reasons from those of 'protest'. On April 10, a book-stealing ring was exposed at an Oxford college. One youth had been corrupted by the prospect of a free copy of Milton's poems. Book-stealing was, in fact, a perennial university problem. The worst offenders were Sussex and Essex.

However, all these minor activities were overshadowed by the events of April 18, just before the university summer term started. Two lecturers were dismissed from the L.S.E. by the Court of

Governors for their part in the destruction of the gates. One of these, a psychology lecturer, had spoken in favour of the destruction of the gates before it took place. The case of the other, a sociology lecturer, was more complicated. He had spoken approvingly of the destruction of the gates just after it occurred. The authorities contended that to approve publicly an act of violence just committed while another—on the forcible exclusion of representatives of firms with interests in Southern Africa—was to be committed (in accordance with the decision of a previous meeting) the following week, was to undermine the principles on which academic institutions are based.

There were vigorously expressed attacks on these dismissals. The Association of University Teachers and the Association of Teachers in Technical Institutions deplored them. 10 L.S.E. professors, led by the Professor of English Law, signed a document demanding an independent enquiry and the suspension of the dismissals until this had taken place. The N.U.S. attacked them as 'atrocious'. A statement by the R.S.S.F. ran: 'The sackings . . . show up the neo-Fascist turn of European capitalism.' Two-thirds of Sussex University teachers signed a letter of protest.

The two lecturers received less support from L.S.E. student body. On April 21 a students' union meeting 'legalized', by 468 votes to 42 with 76 abstentions, the strike and picket already begun by the Socialist Society. The overwhelming majority of L.S.E. students completely ignored this strike. The two lecturers were fortunate to obtain even the support they did receive. At the end of the previous term a meeting convened to protect them from discipline had attracted only 60 or 70 students and had been abandoned.

The continuance of lectures and of student attendance of them compelled the Socialist Society to break them up. This confused many of those, both staff members and students, who had previously been sympathetic to the dismissed lecturers. Union meetings shrank. During the month from April 21 to May 17 there were eight union meetings and many 'general assemblies'. At the first union meeting there were about 600 people present and at the last, about 300.

At an L.S.E. A.U.T. meeting of April 23 there was an unusually high attendance. Normally 20 or 30 attend. On this occasion there were about 150. By 100 votes to 24 with 14 abstentions the meeting demanded an appeals tribunal. By 100 to 33 it asked for the suspension of the dismissals.

At a students' union meeting of the same day, attended by slightly over 500 people, a resolution was carried condemning the strike-breaking actions of an 'anti-democratic minority'. L.S.E. has over 3,000 students. An attempt had, in fact, been made to induce this minority, at least the section of it in the Library, to join the strike. The Extreme Left had sent through the Library a percussion band playing 'Land of Hope and Glory'. This attempt at recruitment had been unsuccessful. Attempts were now made to reach those who did not attend meetings. 'General assemblies' were held in the canteen. As lunches were rendered sparse and finally stopped by the refusal of the Extreme Left to allow food supplies in, the 'general assemblies' aroused little positive response. However, the Extreme Left planned a May Day March which would join the workers' march from Tower Hill. It also planned a National Students' Assembly to be held the following month.

Essex troubles coincided again with L.S.E. ones. On April 24 the visit of the Commons select committee enquiring into student problems was disturbed by a riot in which 70 students took part. They refused to state their case. At Cambridge also there was a disturbance. Windows were broken and Mao's thoughts chanted when Mr. Lee Kuan Yew, the Prime Minister of Singapore, addressed senior members of the University in Senate House.

L.S.E. staff continued to take an interest in domestic politics. Its branch of the A.T.T.I. voted to strike from April 29 and two assistant lecturers in social administration decided to strike at once. On April 25 the academic board met. Of nearly 300 entitled to attend 170 did so—a very high turn-out. Dr. Adams announced that a tribunal was being arranged to review the dismissals. By 98 to 31 the board voted that the dismissals should be suspended until an independent enquiry had been completed or three months had passed. A resolution condemning rowdyism and disturbance of teaching was overwhelmingly carried.

On April 28 another meeting of L.S.E. A.U.T. was held. It attracted fewer people than the previous one had done. By 44 votes to 20 it demanded an independent enquiry.

On April 29 a Conservative party seminar issued some comments on the troubles. Sir Edward Boyle said, 'I believe we are in a period when it will be necessary for more students to be sent down and for a certain number of staff to be dispensed with; but we ought to get the procedure clear.' The seminar accepted the view of Mr. Osband that formal rules and powers of disciplining offenders should be set out in universities. Mr. Ian Taylor, of the executive of the Federation of Conservative Students and an L.S.E. postgraduate, demanded 'firm action'.

Meanwhile the disruption of lectures continued at L.S.E. The governors announced their intention of taking disciplinary action. The Extreme Left announced its intention of bringing the running of the School to a full stop unless the dismissed lecturers were reinstated. However they did not adopt the proposal made after due notice at a union meeting by an anarchist that revolutionary students should burn the L.S.E. down and loot and rape among the smoking ruins. Dr. Adams sent for the student. The student, supported by the Socialist Society in his assertion of his rights, refused to go without legal representation and assistance. This was conceded and the student asserted, at the meeting at which the concession was announced, that the whole meeting of several hundred people constituted this legal representation and assistance.

The visit of the Commons select committee to L.S.E. did not go smoothly. A union meeting had decided against disrupting the proceedings. This decision was ignored and the hard core of the Extreme Left refused to allow Lord Robbins to be questioned by the M.P.s. The Extreme Left did not put its case. Noise, a smoke-bomb and spitting ended the first day of the select committee's hearings at L.S.E. The meeting dissolved as the dismissed sociology lecturer stood on a table and announced that the audience had just witnessed 'a meaningless confrontation'. The second day of the hearing was less eventful. Only 60 staff and students attended. One lecturer, Dr. Terence Morris, reader in sociology with special reference to criminology, told the committee that part of the trouble at L.S.E. was the presence of 'disturbed minds'.

L.S.E. had to face external dangers at this time. On May 4 there was a Conservative rally in Trafalgar Square. Afterwards 400 of the National Front marched on L.S.E. with chants of 'Communists out' and 'We believe in white power'. The police directed the National Front away.

As the Association of Scientific, Technical, Managerial and Administrative Staff was blaming L.S.E. troubles on 'bad management' staff opinion was hardening behind the 'management'. On May 7 an academic board meeting voted, by 125 to 36, for strong measures to deal with disruption and in support of the governors in their execution of such measures. A proposal brought by the Professor of English Law, who had actively supported the strike and had taken the matter to the National Council for Civil Liberties, condemning both disruption and discipline was rejected by 117 to 25. The board voted by 80 to 59 in favour of having students on boards reviewing appeals against disciplinary judgements. The professor proposing this last motion had announced the previous day that he was leaving the L.S.E.

The same day Dr. Adams addressed an audience of 700 students. He had been compelled to do this because a few days earlier he had been introducing a recently promoted professor who was to speak on eighteenth-century history and had had the introduction halted by requests, made through a megaphone, for some future discussion on the L.S.E. troubles. Faced with the prospect of the disruption of an academic occasion Dr. Adams agreed to this proposition and on May 7 in answer to questions on discipline expressed himself clearly: 'Should I let bygones be bygones? I think it would be the act of a coward for me to let down my colleagues, and a public confession that we were not prepared to defend academic freedom and a betrayal of what the School has stood for and stands for.' There was uproar.

The dismissed sociology lecturer had lost some support. In a 'general assembly' of 60 or 70 people he had spoken favourably of the total disruption of all lectures. This was unpopular. Moreover when the Labour Minister, Mr. Richard Crossman, had visited L.S.E. on May 6, the lecturer had tried to talk him down—and this attempt had not been supported.

It must not be supposed that other institutions were entirely quiet at this time. Two Warwick students threatened to boycott their Finals in protest against the examination system. This gesture won more attention than imitation. Southampton University students shouted down Lord Beeching. This had been televised on University Forum and as a result the format of future programmes was changed. However, broadly speaking, L.S.E. Extreme Left was more isolated both inside and outside L.S.E. than it had ever been.

The day after the 'confrontation' with Dr. Adams a union meeting suspended the strike. The opponents of disruption mustered a majority for this meeting, which had an attendance of about 430. Fewer than 200 of the original strikers wished to continue the strike. The disruption of lectures was condemned by about 220 votes to 191. Only the three-weeks-long food picket, in the course of which a van-driver had been assaulted, received retrospective sanction.

The L.S.E. authorities pressed the injunctions obtained after the destruction of the gates and set up a tribunal to discipline those who had disrupted lectures. This was a harder line than that attempted at the same time at Essex, where it was decided to appoint a magistrate and a counsellor to deal with problems and tensions. At Oxford problems of discipline attracted attention too, especially when on May 12 the O.R.S.S. stole a copy of the Hart Report which dealt with these problems. The O.R.S.S. organized a discussion entitled 'Hart or a democratic society?' while the Hebdomadal Council questioned students on their views on the Hart Report. It was discovered that though most junior common room meetings wanted students on disciplinary boards most students questioned individually did not. Thus these institutions reacted in different ways to their difficult minorities.

There was in fact, at London as a whole, a hard line. Sir Douglas Logan advocated the example of those involved in sit-ins. The L.S.E. tried to have some of the disrupters imprisoned. On May 16 this plea was rejected by the judge officiating in the case. The Professor of English Law had testified that the disrupters were 'serious-minded, honest and sincere men who acted as they thought right'. Towards the end of the summer term the L.S.E. disciplinary tribunal suspended three students. It was impossible for the Socialist Society to attract enough students to form a union meeting to protest. The quorum was 60 students. The last active meeting at L.S.E. had been on May 14. This had attracted 300 people and decided to hold a one-day token strike and a march. After this, political action was abandoned for the academic year and when the suspensions were announced nothing was done. Exhaustion and examinations had worn down the forces of destruction.

Examinations, indeed, preoccupied the students of nearly all institutions. When in response to an invitation Mr. Wedgwood Benn, Minister of Technology, visited Bristol University Labour Club on May 23 he found no one to meet him. The examinations had completely if temporarily suppressed any interest in politics. Disturbances moved out of the universities for the moment. There was, however, a 'revolt of working-class youth' at Folkestone. The Mayor described those involved as 'a bunch of spoonfed local yobs'. The chairman of the Young Liberals attempted to hold a 'peoples' assembly' in Downing Street. This attracted about 15 people.

During the relative quiet, negotiation and organization continued in some institutions. At Nottingham it was announced on May 27 that 6 students should sit on the board transacting 95 per cent of the Senate's business. At Cambridge it was proposed that a Tripos of sociology should be set up. This proposal caused an energetically fought battle. On June 10, instead of the usual 150, 800 of Cambridge's senior staff turned out to vote on the issue. By 461 to 332 it was decided to institute such a Tripos.

Meanwhile excitement had subsided at Oxford. The poll of June 3 for the presidency of the Union was the lowest for years. The winner, Mr. Brandreth, obtained 238 votes. Mr. Brandreth's intentions were clear. 'I want to evaporate the greyness in the Union. Let us make glamour and excitement the keynote.' The Union faced a £10,000 deficit.

Excitement at Cambridge subsided too. On June 18 the senior staff voted on the proposal to establish a course of clinical teaching leading to a first medical degree. By 407 to 68 this proposal was carried. Attendance had dropped since the last meeting.

Thus the academic year ended. The government was now spending more on education than on defence. Applications for university were rising and those for Sandhurst falling. The size of the educational problem was now better appreciated. The duties of university teachers were being clarified; the A.U.T. was working out a conduct code for teachers in case of future disputes. Attempts were being made by the N.U.S. to make students take an interest in general politics. This was a hard task. The electoral registration officer dealing with one of the hostels of King's College, London, was puzzled by the surprisingly low incidence of registration. Attempts to form student voting blocks in towns were largely unsuccessful. The year had in fact ended in apathy—and in an intensification of the pressures which would lead to more disturbance. On July 2 the Sociology Association issued a statement denying the responsibility of their subject for university disruption. Possibly its members foresaw what was to come.

During the long vacation of 1969 the memory of the troubles was kept alive by some minor incidents, some of which were portents for the coming academic year. Eton and Harrow were both the subjects of attention by the Schools Action Union which was a junior version of the R.S.S.F. The Black Paper was attacked again and a Red Paper compiled to answer it. The Young Liberals disrupted cricket and tennis matches in which South African teams took part. A Sheffield student who had moved from the Young Conservatives to the Welsh Nationalists to the Anarchists and then out again received four years in gaol for making a bomb for the Investiture of the Prince of Wales. The L.S.E. authorities issued a new set of rules and began the year's handbook with the bold assertion that university institutions were for work and learning. They also forbade a group called the 'Living School' to hold a live-in at L.S.E. The 'Living School' was too weak and ill-supported to hope to force its way in and deliberate in L.S.E. At the beginning of August the L.S.E. examination results were published and from them it was obvious that most of the leaders of the Extreme Left would not be returning. On August 21 the independent tribunal reviewing the dismissal of the sociology lecturer announced that the authorities had been justified. It was clear that the focus of any disturbances in 1969–70 would not be L.S.E.

Thus the year 1968–1969 had been one of confusion, bitterness and strife in the course of which the boundaries of accepted student misbehaviour had been by stages widened. Opinion inside and outside universities had been polarized or battered into bored indifference. Numbers at student meetings had fluctuated so violently that no decision could be relied on. University authorities had been divided within and subjected to the intense pressures of public opinion from without. They were compelled to cope with an ever-increasing number of students in a period of financial restriction.

During the summer vacation there were no signs that any of these pressures would weaken. The occasions and tendencies that would govern the activities of the student Extreme Left in the following year were already present.

3

Continuing Currents

IN THE period covered by this book there were two currents which flowed continuously and with no sign of weakening. They resulted in a sapping of the institutions which they affected. One development was of relatively minor importance but the other struck at the basic purpose of higher education. One although it took place outside universities showed the essence of one particular factor in the practical problems facing universities. The other took place in universities and affected them vitally.

The first of these currents was that of unrest in the art colleges of Guildford and Hornsey. They had been the scenes of sit-ins in the summer term of 1968 and the reverberations of these occupations continued to disturb them. Indeed while the original occupiers lost interest the Ministry of Education, local trades councils, local and national political parties and trade unions became peripherally involved. The sit-ins had originally started and been given impetus by the belief of many art students that the courses leading to their qualifications were too rigidly structured and taught and that in any case admission to these courses should not be dependent on the acquisition of a set number of O-levels including English. They held that the teacher's task was less to explain than to guide. The entire controversy showed the difficulty of setting courses and assessing competence when the final qualification obtained is of its nature impossible to judge—and difficult to sell. An art qualification cannot be related to the community and its needs as simply or as profitably as a qualification in physical science. A Diploma in Art and Design is not to be compared with a B.Sc. in Maths. In fact the study of art presents the same difficulties and the same temptations as the study of sociology and

48

other subjects not obviously vulnerable to empirical investigation and judgement. An artist's career is as uncertain today as in previous generations, partly because with the bestowal of state grants more people can acquire the basic skills and this intensifies competition for the employment available. The pressures on art students are both stronger and weaker than those on most other students.

The second and more important development of these two years was the attrition of the practice of the presentation of a variety of opinions and interpretations in universities. At the beginning of this period the loud heckling of a visiting politician still aroused surprise and indignation. By the end of it lectures had been disrupted with less reaction or response. There are difficulties in defining disruption of this sort. The purpose of universities for the last few decades has been to collect facts and bring different viewpoints to bear on them to find truth. The core of this process is reading, experimentation, lecturing and being lectured, setting and following courses and so forth. Outside this there are academic occasions, visits by famous scholars, inaugural general addresses, etc. Outside this again, and part of the necessary if extra-curricular activities of a university community, there are discussions of a political nature. These meetings are often attended and addressed by well-known politicians. The purpose of these meetings may often be that of conversion but it is usually hoped by at least some of those present that thought will be stimulated or at least clearly and entertainingly articulated. Over the two years ending in July 1970 disruption reached all three types of university activity in turn, beginning with the political meetings and ending with the lectures.

The year 1968–69 opened with disputes about the readmission of students and reappointment of staff at Guildford and Hornsey. At Guildford one student who had been involved in the previous term's sit-in was after pressure from her parents readmitted. On the first day of term 30 of 45 dismissed staff were on picket-duty. Hornsey did not start term till a month after the usual date. Attempts were made to arouse and re-arouse feeling. On October 5 there was a demonstration on behalf of art college students in Trafalgar Square. There were pop-songs and poetry-readings on the programme. The demonstration attracted about 1,000 people.

The same week, Guildford trade council demanded an enquiry into the dispute at the Guildford School of Art, now renamed the Guildford School of Design. This was in accordance with a decision taken at a meeting of Guildford School of Art Student-Staff Association.

None of this impressed either the local or the college authorities. On October 11 Surrey county council announced that seven Guildford teachers were to be dismissed for their part in the previous term's occupation. The N.U.S. protested. Mr. Straw of the N.U.S. executive forecast that unless enquiries were held into these disputes many art colleges were likely to be disturbed. Sir John Summerson, chairman of the National Commission for Diplomas in Art and Design, on which one of Hornsey's dissenting staff had just accepted a seat, deplored the dismissals. Plans were made to lobby M.P.s. A Labour county councillor, Mr. Tony Heath, expressed his view frankly: 'The people responsible who are wasting ratepayers' money in this way are not fit to be in charge of spending.' Another councillor, Mr. John Strudwick, blamed the principal and governors for the 'mess'. Feelings were not soothed by the offer of £10,000 in compensation for 32 of the staff dispersed for non-disciplinary reasons.

A deputation of Guildford students were to serenade Mr. Short, the Education Minister. Three of them were allowed to see him and give him a message. Guildford was 'blacked' by the Association of Teachers in Technical Institutions. Thus even before the end of October 1968 it was obvious that there was little spirit of reconciliation.

Meanwhile Hornsey had been preparing for the term. The authorities decided to distribute grants in monthly instalments. They also fortified the college ready for reopening. One of the dissenting staff said,

> They are even putting grilles on the windows. The governors have succeeded in turning a building which once had the free air of an art school into a fortified approved school. If they have spent all that ratepayers' money to thwart another sit-in, which is what we suspect, then it has all been a waste . . . next time we will make our point in a different way.

As this quotation suggests the opposition to the governors was organizing itself. An ex-president of Hornsey students' union had published on October 8 an article claiming that in the previous term's sit-in 700 students had taken part, that 600 residents had signed a petition in favour of the sit-in and that the sit-in had been supported by the local Labour, Liberal and Communist parties. A motion was brought by the Labour opposition before Haringey Council to the effect that an independent enquiry into the dissensions should be instituted. This motion was rejected. The activist students then arranged for a mass meeting to be held to discuss the cases of 18 students dismissed for academic reasons. The chairman of the education committee commented, 'I can assure the students that the dismissals were perfectly genuine.' He denied that there was a policy of weeding out the troublemakers.

Apart from staff and student dismissals the most likely cause of the continuance of strife at Hornsey was the difference between the opinion of the governing body and that of the staff-student commission, chaired by Lord Longford, on the number of students who should sit on the academic panel which was a vital component of the school's administration. The staff-student commission recommended seven; the governing body thought that two was enough.

Plans were considered, therefore, to picket the college with and for the dismissed students. Plans were also made for a large meeting. Another sit-in was considered. The meeting was held on November 1 at Enfield Technical College and attended by 200 students. Nothing was definitely decided.

The two dozen dismissed Hornsey students expected to return with the 700 accepted ones. It should be remembered that the fall in applications which followed the sit-in had reduced the student body by about 100. Alderman Cathles of the local council said that the two dozen students would not be returning. However, the college opened peacefully. This peace was very brief indeed.

On November 4, almost before staff and students had settled in, they debated the new academic structure of the institution. The debate was interrupted by about 60 students from Goldsmiths' College who invaded the meeting with chants of 'We support you'. This support was not welcomed.

On the same day Guildford had entirely internal disturbances.

50 students decided to sit-in to protest against the 'savage victimization' of the dismissals. This can hardly have cheered the authorities; the previous sit-in had cost £5,000. However, the sit-in ended the next day.

Hornsey was keeping in step. Lord Longford told an enthusiastic audience of students that he disapproved very much of the governing body's dismissal of staff. 'I must say that is no way to run a college, or whelk-stall for that matter.' The response of the chairman of the governing body, Alderman Lawrence Bains, was terse. He warned that further disturbances might lead to closure.

On November 7 both colleges were again affected by outside intervention. Three dozen Brighton and Sussex students appeared in Guildford refectory at lunch-time to protest against the dismissal of staff. They carried banners with the message 'Reinstate the purged staff'. The unasked-for assistance from Brighton students was not appreciated. A poster was hung out of the window with the injunction 'Go home, Brighton'. The police were called and the Brighton students were evicted. Student solidarity was distinctly parochial on this occasion, as it had been a few days earlier at Hornsey.

In the case of Hornsey the external intervention of November 7 was of a different type. Mr. Norman Atkinson, Labour M.P. for Tottenham, asked Mrs. Shirley Williams of the Department of Education and Science for an enquiry into the Hornsey disputes. He complained that Lord Longford had received 'shabby treatment'.

The following day 20 Hornsey students who had failed their assessments and been denied readmission on those grounds were readmitted on a two-month probationary period. However, 8 others were again refused readmission. On November 11 the N.U.S. Executive demanded an enquiry into the educational standards of Guildford and Hornsey.

On the same day Mr. John Pardoe, Liberal spokesman on education in the House of Commons, demanded an enquiry into the Guildford dispute. He claimed that Surrey education committee 'manages with unfailing regularity to give the impression of being composed of a load of high-ranking bemedalled and much-titled ne'er-do-wells, whose sole criterion of a good education is a short back-and-sides . . . nasty right-wing politics'. It must be made clear that the local authorities in charge of Hornsey and Guildford were Conservative.

Some interest from outside was more easily understandable. On November 13 130 parents of students had a meeting with Mr. Arnold, the principal of Guildford. They were led by the father of the student who had been readmitted after some pressure. After the meeting this father said, 'Mr. Arnold has refused to answer my questions relevant to the sit-in, the sacking of staff and the happenings at the School.' A week later, on November 19, 200 Guildford students marched to the Department of Education and Science to demand an enquiry. Thus tension was maintained.

Also on November 19 a meeting of Hornsey students instructed two of their number to enquire into the evidence on which the dismissals of their eight colleagues had been based. By this time a fresh cause of confusion was appearing for Haringey education committee had just decided to merge Hornsey with the technical institutions of Hendon and Enfield to form a polytechnic.

The next week contained the N.U.S. autumn conference at Margate. This supported 'direct action' by the art college students, demanded that art colleges should be removed from the control of local authorities and asked for an enquiry. By the end of November the A.T.T.I., too, was involving itself more actively in these disputes and considering black-listing, in addition to Guildford, all the further education colleges in Surrey. Surrey county council did not seem alarmed.

On December 9 the president of Hornsey students' union said, 'We are discussing the possibility of more demonstrations after Christmas.' He objected to the changes in administration planned by the governing body. The following day Alderman Cathles defended the changes, 'What we are proposing is that the principal should have the powers he has always had and that he should report to the college executive. The purpose is to bring the executive in line with points raised by students.' It must be said that by this time the governing body had adopted the recommendation that seven students should sit on the academic panel.

On December 10 Hornsey's new regulations for discipline were carried by Haringey council despite the opposition of the Labour minority. 20 students shouting in the gallery were threatened with removal. The internal secretary of the students' union commented,

'These new regulations are a step backwards. They give more power to the principal to suspend students and do not allow students the right of appeal to any body on which either staff or students are represented.'

On December 11 matters took a different turn at Guildford. 50 students complained that the three representatives who were to meet the Commons select committee of enquiry were all 'militants'. However, this resistance was brief. The next matter to agitate the institution occurred two days later. It was discovered that the letters informing the students' parents of the proposed amalgamation of the school had not been sent. There had been a mistake. In the midst of these harassments the principal must have been glad to hear that Professor MacIntyre of Essex University, who had investigated Guildford's Department of Complementary Studies in March, had thought it 'very good'. Guildford was not to suffer the same loss of academic esteem as Hornsey.

Hornsey indeed was about to lose some of its staff. Four of its part-timers were dismissed on December 15 for encouraging the sitters-in of the previous term. One said, 'This is collective liquidation. We are being massacred.' Alderman Lawrence Bains saw it differently. 'It is pointless for every temporary member of the staff whose contract is not renewed to cry victimization. We shall not be persuaded from making changes in college courses by moral blackmail of this kind.' The head of the Art History and Complementary Studies Department maintained that he was completely taken by surprise by these dismissals. He feared gross understaffing.

Some students planned to disrupt the next meeting of the academic panel and on December 18 the president of the students' union with 50 others invaded this meeting of the panel, 7 of whose 26 members were students, and asked: 'Is this meeting open to observers? Was it consulted over the sacking of four members of the academic staff?' After this disruption he complained that the authorities '. . . treated us like children. Students are very dissatisfied and I can see only a very bleak future next term. The only course open to us is direct action and it seems likely that the college will close'. On December 19 a students' meeting demanded the resignation of the principal, Mr. Shelton. 202 students signed a statement of protest about the running of the school. However this was not enough to make an effective occupation and there were not enough students to resort to disruption on a large scale. It was also the end of term.

The year 1969 opened quietly for these art colleges. Indeed, until February 13, they sank from public notice. On this date, however, Guildford students' union voted to re-employ some of the dismissed staff and pay for these unofficial classes out of union funds.

In April the N.U.S. held its Easter conference. The president of Hornsey students' union made a long speech on the art college disputes. There were balloons, klaxons and confetti. There was also the symbolic assassination of two students called 'hope' and 'sanity'. The president received an ovation. On April 1 there had been a march of 250 Hornsey students in mourning for their lost hopes.

The conference gave overwhelming support to a motion proposing a National Day of Student Action for art colleges on May 28, the anniversary of the end of the Hornsey sit-in. The power of the N.U.S. over the 400,000 students of Britain was soon to be shown by their response to this motion. It was claimed that the A.T.T.I. boycott of Guildford was effective.

Attempts were made to encourage co-operation and good feeling in these institutions. The Hornsey Commission suggested on April 25 that staff and students should be consulted before major decisions were taken. It also suggested the willing provision of information 'so that communities can become communities of understanding'. This hope was vain.

Attempts at agitation were not successful either. On May 20 Mr. Jack Straw, new president of the N.U.S., claimed that students' unions' presidents who were elected by up to 70 per cent of their students had more right to act in the names of their unions than local councillors who were elected on a 25 per cent poll had to act in the names of their boroughs and counties.

The following day a three-hour student meeting at Guildford resulted in a decision by 73 votes to 17 for occupation in order to force the institution of an independent enquiry. One spokesman said, 'We shall work as usual while we are sitting-in.' This sit-in lasted for a week.

On the same day Mr. Straw attacked apathy. Of 20,000 students in Manchester 70 attended the meeting and march intended to begin the National Week of Student Action to compel the government to hold an enquiry into the disputes at Hornsey and Guildford. However a protest note was handed in as planned.

At the end and climax of the Week of Action Mr. Straw made a speech accusing Hornsey authorities of trying to wage a campaign of attrition:

> All are suffering in an atmosphere of disillusion and depression. Some have found the strain too much. There are persistent rumours which we are trying our best to substantiate that during the year there have been nine suicide attempts and 42 nervous breakdowns.

Of Mr. Short, the Minister of Education, Mr. Straw said, 'He must do something about the real thugs of the situation, the local authorities of Surrey and Haringey.' Mr. Straw led 2,000 people on a march to the Department of Education and Science. This number sank to about 700 when led to Speakers' Corner afterwards.

Mr. Shelton, principal of Hornsey, commented:

> It's a great pity that Mr. Jack Straw made no effort to consult me before making a speech containing several blatantly incorrect statements. It is not true that staff have been dismissed as part of a campaign of attrition by the authorities. We normally have a large staff turnover. This year we have had to lay off staff because there are about 80 fewer students at Hornsey, but the reason for this was the student sit-in last year which adversely affected recruiting and the many withdrawals at the college as a result of students' actions. Whatever disruption and reduction in size there is at Hornsey is a result of student action. This applies also to the unsettling atmosphere at Hornsey now. Students have had political pressure put on them and have been press-ganged to take part in demonstrations.

Mr. Shelton also stated that there were only ten students under psychiatric treatment and that some of these cases dated from before the sit-in. He concluded with the assertion that to the best of his knowledge there had only been two suicide attempts, both of which were made by students who had made attempts before the sit-in.

Thus the year ended in anti-climax at both colleges. There had been many small and ill-supported disturbances rather than one massive one in each college. The authorities, both local and college, had maintained, in the words of Surrey county council in November 1968, that 'an important duty of members of staff is to set an example to their students by their observance of law and order'.

The next academic year followed the same pattern though the initial impetus had gone. On October 3, 1969 a student previously expelled from Guildford was readmitted as his assessments proved satisfactory. On October 28 Surrey county council rejected a proposal calling for an enquiry into the Guildford dismissals. On December 21 the Summerson council decided that Hornsey's Dip.A.D. courses should not be recognized for the normal five years. The Council had not been impressed by its investigation in the previous term on the state of Dip.A.D. studies at Hornsey. This blow to Hornsey's reputation made its projected union with Hendon and Enfield Colleges of Technology to form a polytechnic less likely of fulfilment.

The Files Controversy left both institutions untouched but in March 1970 Hornsey students' union sent to the local authorities a vote of no confidence in the principal and the chairman of the governing body. The union's reason was the non-renewal of the contract of a teacher involved in the sit-in of 1968. The union claimed that the teacher had been dismissed 'on political grounds'. Hornsey union was also at this time threatening to boycott negotiations with the authorities unless new machinery of representation was introduced.

Meanwhile at the Farnham Centre of the West Surrey College of Art and Design, as Guildford had become, 137 signed a petition asking Mr. Short to hold a public independent enquiry into the past and present situation of the college.

During this month Hornsey union also voted, at a meeting of about 200, to ask the N.U.S. at its next conference to blacklist Hornsey. The same meeting voted for student representation on boards employing and dismissing staff, for a more effective information service within the college, for a lifting of the confidentiality rules at meetings of the governing body and for a boycott of the department of the recently dismissed teacher. West Surrey College of Art and Design union also prepared a similar

3

motion for the N.U.S. The Easter N.U.S. conference adopted these proposals.

The dispute showed renewed signs of affecting other bodies. In April 1970 30 people, including Mr. Tony Heath, a Labour member of the county council, Mr. John Fahy, secretary of the Guildford trades council, Mr. Digby Jacks, of the N.U.S. executive, Surrey University students, West Surrey College students and some of the dismissed staff, handed out leaflets to schoolchildren. These leaflets advised the children not to apply to West Surrey College of Art and Design.

The Surrey Association for the Advancement of State Education agreed to circulate N.U.S. blacklist pamphlets to its six branches. The Guildford trades council sent leaflets to its 40 components. The N.U.S. claimed that applications to the two colleges were falling as a result of public criticism. What the public were criticizing was not stated. Representatives of several unions with members employed by Surrey county council met to consider possible action to force either an enquiry or the reinstatement of dismissed staff. All these forms of agitation failed to achieve their ostensible purpose. Leaflets could be sent out and meetings held but they could not compel obedience.

This stage of the disputes split Hornsey along occupational lines. 180 of 200 Hornsey staff signed a protest against the N.U.S. blacklisting. By 101 to 52 the students' union voted to ratify the blacklist. Attendance at this meeting suggested weakening interest.

By June 1970 the Summerson council again showed concern about Hornsey's academic worth. The Coldstream Report on art education was received with complaints and indifference. Dissatisfaction remained an undercurrent in the art institutions. The hope expressed by one Hornsey student in December 1968 had been: 'This means real responsibility. To fight for reforms is one thing, but to carry them out is even more demanding. The sit-in was pure joy because we learnt we all felt the same, we were totally involved. Now it's a case of making things work we believe in. It's a subtle marvellous change.'

The second continuing development over the two years 1968–70 was more serious. It affected the very foundation of higher education. Variety of opinion was eroded. Disruption of speeches at meetings, which had previously been exceptional, now became common. This trend included another which was only to reach full development in 1969–70. This was the extension of student rights of veto from university activities to public activities.

This aspect in fact was the first to appear in the two years 1968–70. On October 7, 1968 the inaugural disruption of the year took place. It occurred at Oxford and ended in the abandonment of a meeting of the Society for Individual Freedom. The Press had been informed beforehand that the meeting would not be quiet. The guest speakers at this meeting, Mr. Ronald Bell, Conservative M.P. for South Buckinghamshire, and Sir Ian MacTaggart, Conservative former councillor, attacked the Race Relations Act. This occasioned disturbance. The demonstrators elected their own chairman of the meeting, a member of All Soul's College, and sang the 'Internationale'. It seemed that they were unsure of the words. The meeting closed amid cries of 'Here come the fuzz'.

On the same day Cambridge University announced that it was unwilling to have Mr. Powell on university property. It feared that a meeting addressed by him might lead to a disturbance. However the chairman of Cambridge Conservative Association continued to plan a visit by Mr. Powell. The visit was arranged for October 27 —the day of the Vietnam Demonstration. 'We hope,' said the chairman of the Conservative Association, 'that the rough elements will go to London, and we shall be left with the moderates to deal with.'

The next student commotion provided an omen of intervention in the public's choice of entertainment. On October 12 the police were called to a Leicester cinema where students were disturbing the showing of the film *The Green Berets*. This film was sympathetic to the American armies in Vietnam.

On October 23 Mr. Powell addressed an audience of 2,000 students at Exeter University. 30 or 40 people shouted Mr. Powell down. The majority of those present voted to let him continue. However the disrupters ignored this vote. Mr. Powell's views on the balance of payments remained unheard, if not unexpressed. His offer to take his opponents on in a question and answer session was refused. His opponents threw marbles. Later the guild executive of the students' union deplored this disruption. The Federation of

Conservative Students issued a statement. 'The Federation hopes that no university or college Conservative Association will in the future cancel any meetings with Mr. Powell as a result of this incident. Responsible students must stand up against all those who seek to destroy the right of free speech in our universities.' Mr. Powell's right to speak at Exeter was also defended by the Labour M.P., Sir Geoffrey de Freitas.

On October 25 Mr. Powell addressed an audience of 500 at Reading. With difficulty he made himself heard to the end. However some had obviously taken the view of the Exeter student who had said, 'If people listen to this man they are only encouraging his fascist racial policies.'

On October 27 Mr. Powell was smuggled into Cambridge Union. Hundreds of students stayed away from the Vietnam Demonstration to picket him. Their efforts were in vain. He asked for the Press to be excluded from the meeting.

On October 29 the students' union of Leeds University voted by 222 to 173 to allow Major Patrick Wall, Conservative M.P. for Haltemprice, to come and address the university's Conservative Association. Leeds had previously been the scene of a student riot in the course of which Major Wall's wife had been kicked.

On November 8 Mr. Powell addressed an audience in Cardiff. Several dozen people, led by the local Labour M.P., Mr. North, walked out loudly. Others briefly prevented Mr. Powell from leaving.

This, however, was very mild, particularly when compared to the receptions given to Major Wall, who no longer brought his wife to meetings, at Leeds and York and to Mr. Powell himself at Bath. These incidents also took place on November 8.

At Leeds the disrupters distributed leaflets to the audience telling it in what order to make certain types of disturbance. This programme included the singing of 'Rule, Britannia', 'five minutes' spontaneous laughter', 'one minute's silence in memory of his good lady wife', 'three minutes' footstamping' and a chorus of 'I'm dreaming of a white Christmas'. 1,500 students attended this meeting.

At York later Major Wall addressed 400 students on Rhodesia. His speech could not be heard, 30 or 40 students stormed the platform and cut the microphone. Some wore swastika armbands.

Meanwhile Mr. Powell was addressing 2,000 people at Bath University on the implications of the Fulton Report on the civil service. He was greeted with cheers and howls and his speech was rendered difficult to hear by brawls and cries of 'fascist!' and 'nazi!' After the meeting students lay down in front of his car as they had done at Cardiff.

For a short time the focus of attention shifted from Mr. Powell and Major Wall. On November 13 Sir Cyril Osborne, Conservative M.P. for Louth, addressed an audience at Oxford on 'The Profit Motive'. The meeting was disturbed by shouts and scuffles.

During the already-mentioned sit-in at the London Inns of Court the first example was provided of interference by some students with the work of other students. Non-occupying students were physically prevented from going to tutorials by the students in occupation. 'I want to qualify at the Bar, not mess about with this kind of nonsense' was ignored.

On November 17 it was shown that Reading University was not going to provide occasion for disturbance. It decided not to hold a public welcoming ceremony for 30 U.S.A. girl students. Not only political and academic but also social activities were to be circumscribed.

On November 20 it was announced that Sheffield University students' union had forbidden the Conservative Association to invite Mr. Powell to address it. The explanation was, 'We could not guarantee his safety or security. I fear he could be manhandled by left-wing elements.' On the same day such an 'undemocratic spirit' was shown at a Manchester University students' union meeting to a proposal to invite Mr. Powell to the institution that the Conservative Association decided to postpone any such invitation.

On November 20 Mr. Powell addressed the Monday Club and expressed himself frankly on student unrest and conciliatory vice-chancellors. This did not increase his popularity in universities. On the following day the Prime Minister, Mr. Wilson, answered a parliamentary complaint about the treatment meted out to Mr. Powell in these words: 'I am much in favour of free speech at universities and everywhere else, for all forms of opinion, but in view of the way Mr. Powell has clothed his utterly evil proposals, I am not surprised he provokes some reaction.'

The day afterwards 'some reaction' was shown at Exeter University where Mr. Powell addressed another meeting. Mr. Powell was greeted by students wearing golliwog masks. There were the by now customary expressions of criticism. On the same day it transpired that for security reasons Mr. Powell would be unable to take part in a radio programme to be recorded in Oxford.

Meanwhile Major Wall was to address Southampton University Conservative Association. The Extreme Left had failed, despite several attempts, to persuade the students' union to forbid this. The authorities had refused him permission to speak in the University Hall and had recommended that he speak on student property. On November 25 he was smuggled in to address his audience. He was shouted down. There were cries of 'Black and white, unite and fight!' and 'Racialism out!' During a lull Major Wall enquired, 'Come on, what's wrong?' Of them, he said, 'They have more lungs than brains. Their conduct is more fitting to a primary school than a university.' He received a standing ovation from most students.

On November 28 the chairman of Bradford University Conservative Association publicly complained that on November 10 Bradford students' union council had forbidden any university society to invite Mr. Powell. The issue was soon put to the test. On December 3 Bradford called off a meeting to be addressed by a local councillor who had opposed the wearing of traditional headdress by Sikh bus-conductors.

Attention now moved to more central political figures. On November 29 Mr. Heath, leader of the Conservative Party, was shouted down at Swansea University College. On December 4 Mr. Roy Jenkins, Home Secretary in the Labour Government, was shouted down at the University of East Anglia. There was bellowing and slow hand-clapping. The cause of complaint was British policy in the Nigerian civil war. Only a few dozen of the hundreds present disrupted the meeting. Mr. Jenkins said, 'I would be grateful if you would not try your bullying fascist tactics on me.' At the end of term there was an anti-Powell pageant.

On the same day it was announced that Mr. Powell would not be able to speak at his old school in Birmingham on 'Gold, Money and the Balance of Payments'. The local university was in a state of turmoil due to an occupation. The bailiff of Mr. Powell's old school said, 'In view of the disorderly conditions now prevailing at the University of Birmingham and of threats made by extremists from this and other universities to invade the premises and disrupt the meeting, we have reluctantly felt compelled to rule that the meeting cannot be held at present.' It must be remarked that occupations caused great concern to local inhabitants for reasons suggested in this quotation.

On December 5 the student right of veto was extended to academic lectures. L.S.E. provided this precedent. Professor Trevor-Roper was to give the lecture, entitled 'The Past and the Present', for Oration Day. The Extreme Left posted up copies of an article he had written on the regime in Greece and demanded that instead of giving his lecture he should have a 'discussion' with L.S.E. students on Greece. The leaders of the Extreme Left read through Professor Trevor-Roper's writings in the library and found some expressions sympathetic to South Vietnam. These too they publicized in the hope that they would arouse feelings of hostility. Confrontation was avoided, to the open disappointment of some of the Extreme Left, by the compromise of allowing the Professor to give his lecture and then allowing the Left to have a 'discussion' with him. This 'discussion' consisted of long rhetorical questions addressed to Professor Trevor-Roper with choruses of 'Answer!' from most of the gathering.

On the same day Sussex University students' union decided to forbid Mr. Powell or any other with such views on race to speak at the university. Simultaneously a graduate of the university complained that the local authorities would not employ him as a teacher because of his part in the paint-throwing incident of the previous year. He had thus been compelled to become a bus-conductor.

The following day Mr. Powell addressed a meeting of 500 people at Wolverhampton College of Technology. 100 of these screamed at him. 30 marched round the hall with a banner reading 'Walk out on Enoch'. He threatened to leave if the noise did not stop in two minutes. He carried out this threat. To reporters he said, 'You must say what you think.' The president of the students' union apologized to Mr. Powell on behalf of the students as a whole.

On December 9 Mr. Jeger, Labour M.P. for Goole, refused an

invitation to speak at Hull because he felt strongly about the reception given to Major Wall at Leeds.

On December 10 Professor Bernard Williams, giving the yearly Foundation Oration at Birbeck College, London, warned of the possible mutation of universities from academic to political institutions. He mentioned L.S.E. in particular. The next term was to show that there was substance in his fears.

Mr. Short, the Minister for Education, took a more optimistic view. 'I am not advocating anarchy. What I am advocating is the transformation of authority by making this "autonomous conscience" its motive power. Only if this is done can there be any creative individual advances in standards of behaviour.' He was soon to see some noticeable developments of the 'autonomous conscience'.

The attitudes of those responsible for the disruption of meetings in 1968 can be summed up in a few quotations. In *Chips*, the student magazine of the University of East Anglia, one student wrote: 'The tactics employed by the more enlightened students present were indeed the only course of action which could be effective.' In the Sussex University student paper, the editor wrote: '. . . throwing red paint at a minor American official, which was condemned by the majority of the students' union, got attention from everyone and columns of coverage in the States. It may actually have influenced by its shock value.' A Sussex post-graduate said: 'It's possible that the five or so reactionaries in this university could have listened to Enoch Powell in peace, but we did not choose to let them.'

The next term was a logical continuation of its predecessor. On January 15, 1969 200 students at the Rutherford College of Technology, Newcastle-on-Tyne, started a sit-in to prevent Mr. Powell from coming to the college to speak on 'Gold, Money and Politicians'. This sit-in was the climax of a week of agitation by the local Labour Party, including its minority group on the local council, and the Campaign Against Racial Discrimination. These groups had protested against the decision of the college governors to give Mr. Powell a platform. The principal, Mr. Elliott, was believed to have told students that he would call the police if the lecture were disrupted. A door check was planned. Some of the students opposed to Mr. Powell wanted not to stop him coming but to make him have a question-and-answer session. Newcastle University students interested themselves in the dispute. About 100 of them attended a meeting at which a vote of censure was passed on the vice-chancellor, Dr. Henry Miller, for agreeing to take the chair at the meeting to be addressed at Rutherford College by Mr. Powell.

On January 16 the principal and the registrar announced that the meeting was cancelled. The sitters-in went away. Mr. Powell was then smuggled in. The sitters-in came back. There was a disturbance in which the local communists and university students took a prominent part.

The previous day a meeting at Middlesbrough College of Technology at which Mr. Powell had been due to speak had been cancelled because of threats of militant action. However, resistance to measures of this nature was still being offered by some students' unions. At the Regent Street Polytechnic a proposal to deny recruiting facilities to firms with interests in South Africa and Rhodesia was defeated. A demonstration in support of such exclusion attracted about 20 students.

On January 17 Mr. Powell addressed the Conservative Association of Sheffield University. Since the students' union had forbidden him to speak at the university he delivered his speech at the Grand Hotel. 400 student opponents of Mr. Powell stood outside the hotel and tried to persuade him to come out and have a discussion with them. He refused. There were 100 police outside the hotel and 20 inside. After about half an hour Mr. Powell's opponents went away. Earlier in the same day Mr. Powell had been guarded by police and dogs when he addressed a gathering of Conservative women in the Merchant Taylors' Hall, York, where some students picketed the gates.

Meanwhile there were apprehensions about Mr. Powell's planned visit to Oxford. There the local Committee for Racial Integration asked the city and university authorities to prevent Mr. Powell from addressing the university's Conservative Association in the Town Hall. The speech was to be on 'University Pay'. A '20th January Committee' was formed. It enjoined the 'thousands of Oxford workers and students' to prevent the meeting. On January 18 Mr. Eldon Griffiths, a prominent Conservative, told Newmarket Conservative Association that, if university teachers could not ensure the safety of guest speakers, then new administrators should be found. He said, 'Mr. Powell has surely just as much right to offer his opinion as anyone else in the country. His views are of a great deal more interest—and importance—than those of a rabble of downy-faced youths with the marks of the cradle still on them.' Opinion was hardening.

On January 20 Mr. Powell spoke at Oxford. 300 or 400 of his student critics struggled outside with the police who separated them from 150 members of the student Group for Order and Democracy. Ticket-holders only were allowed in to hear Mr. Powell and after the meeting a decoy car was used to ensure his unmolested departure. At this meeting Mr. Powell said that he was in favour of the proposed Independent University.

On January 23 Mrs. Williams, Secretary of State at the Department of Education and Science, addressed Bristol University Labour Club. She opposed the concept of the Independent University. She put her view of Mr. Powell's addresses to universities as follows: 'There are some people—and I suspect Mr. Powell is among them—in whose interests it is that every university they visit erupts into demonstrations, the wilder the better. It is not the Enoch Powells who are being harmed by this, it is the students. Every time they fall for such well-planned provocation, not only students but universities too suffer in the eyes of the public.' This warning went unheeded.

On January 27 a more powerful voice was heard on the issue. Mr. Wilson, the Prime Minister, publicly defended the decision of Bradford University governing body that Mr. Powell should be allowed to speak at the university.

Less well-known people suffered from disruption of their speeches to university meetings. On February 10 Mr. Ian Taylor, chairman of the Federation of Conservative Students, was assaulted by a Left-wing student at Newcastle University.

Some authorities took a hard line. On February 20 the court of governors of Birmingham University voted overwhelmingly against a motion brought by student representatives to the effect that Mr. Powell should be removed from the court. They did not believe that the composition of the court should be influenced by political considerations.

On February 24 Major Wall addressed the Conservative Asso

ciation at Portsmouth College of Technology. The microphone cable was torn. Major Wall was soaked by the contents of a fire-extinguisher.

Meanwhile Oxford was still feeling the effects of Mr. Powell's visit. 24 demonstrators had been fined. Mr. Sutcliffe, a Fellow of Jesus College, was running a staff appeal fund to pay these fines. He obtained £60 from 30 dons.

The next incident in which Major Wall was involved was at the London School of Economics. There some members of the Conservative Association took the view that the January teach-in on Rhodesia had not adequately presented the case of the Monday Club. So they held their own teach-in addressed by Major Wall and Mr. Biggs-Davison, Conservative M.P. for Chigwell. Attempts were made to mislead the Left about the time of this meeting. The London University Section of the Officer Training Corps was called upon to provide protection for the speakers. This proved a necessary precaution. The meeting closed in disorder after the by now customary seizure of the microphone.

The next erosion of variety of opinion also occurred at the London School of Economics. It was the disruption of academic lectures and was the logical consequence of the tolerance extended implicitly and explicitly to the disruption of political meetings and academic gatherings. The principal victim of these disruptions of lectures was Professor Alan Day. He was shouted down with obscenities. His lecture notes were scattered and he had a glass of water poured over him by a non-student present. Those who had come to hear him lecture on economics heard instead a speech from the Socialist Society deputy president of the union.

Other types of disruption continued. At the Commons select committee hearing at Essex, the microphones were seized. One student said, 'You don't mean anything to us, you are bloody irrelevant.' One put a floppy hat on the head of an M.P. At the afternoon session of this hearing a student rose and started a speech beginning 'Comrades . . .' Mr. Longden, the M.P. chairing the session, said that he would give the audience one minute to decide whether evidence was to be given. On the expiry of this minute the student showed no signs of stopping so the M.P.s and the vice-chancellor left to continue the hearing in quieter conditions. They had to step over students' bodies to get out. As has already been described this committee had similar troubles at L.S.E. The disruption of these hearings made it clear no independent enquiry into student unrest would be permitted by the Extreme Left. Variety of opinion among enquirers as well as speakers was considered out of the question. Mr. Jack Straw commented, 'It is intolerable and inexcusable for students to treat select committee members like this. Students at the other 23 colleges visited by the committee welcomed the unique opportunity to present their views to an independent and open-minded committee.' He made no suggestion on how to deal with situations of this type.

Once more politicians became the centre of the controversy over the presentation of differing views. As already mentioned, Lord Beeching was shouted down at Southampton. Mr. Powell once more became an occasion of contention. He had been invited to speak on May 10 on economic matters to Aston University Conservative Association. The meeting had been intended for the students' union building. However, a sit-in by 100 students, including some from L.S.E., prevented this. Mr. Powell gave his speech to 200 Conservatives. He had a hostile reception from about 400. Stinkbombs were thrown. Mr. Powell was protected by 25 rugby players. After the meeting the president of the students' union said that the bill for damages would go to the Socialist Society and that discipline would be considered. On this occasion Mr. Powell said that he would not address any more meetings at redbrick universities but might consider visiting Oxford and Cambridge.

On May 23 the Duke of Edinburgh addressed a Scottish audience. He told a persistent student heckler to shut up and grow up. He said, 'Freedom of speech has not been invented in the last five years. People have been arguing and dying for freedom of speech for a great deal longer than that. There are a lot of people who believe in it very strongly. I know I do . . . Freedom is not licence.'

With these two episodes the academic year 1968–69 ended. The following year saw the consolidation and extension of the ground gained by the forces of this attrition. The sole effective punishment for disruption of this kind had been the suspension of three L.S.E. students. In one case the suspension had itself been suspended while in the other two cases the students concerned were already at the end of their final year. One received a lower second and one, a third. They would not therefore have qualified for government grants for L.S.E. Graduate School.

The next year saw slightly fewer episodes of this kind. In some cases intimidation was effective. In October 1969 Birmingham University United Nations Association invited one of the National Front to give an address on 'Overseas Aid'. Birmingham Extreme Left compelled the U.N.A. to cancel this invitation.

On October 21 the vice-chancellor of Oxford University, Mr. Alan Bullock, found it impossible at times to make himself heard during the matriculation ceremonies. There were chants of 'Matriculation makes a man of you'.

On October 28 100 students started to sit-in at the Cambridge Union in order to prevent Mr. Powell from coming to speak on nationalization. Mr. Hugh Anderson, president of the Union and a member of the Labour Party, commented, 'We utterly deplore this restriction of the right to free speech.' The following day, or rather night, 400 Cambridge students held a torchlight procession in protest against Mr. Powell's visit.

Mr. Powell's popularity in the country and unpopularity in the universities increased still further on November 11 when, as he had often been challenged to do, he expounded his views on immigration in the House of Commons. Once more he was both contributor to and catalyst of polarization. However in the autumn term and for most of the spring term he occasioned little trouble among students. This was partly because most Extreme Left-wing activists were involved in the Springbok Tour and the Files Controversy.

Both of these episodes were the occasion of disturbance. On November 26 the car of the South African ambassador was attacked in Newcastle-on-Tyne. Violence was not confined to South African Springboks matches. The Files Controversy gave rise to the disruption of lectures. The vice-chancellor of Sussex University, Professor Asa Briggs, was shouted down when he attempted to give a lecture. He was compelled, after finally being allowed to give his lecture, to 'discuss' the files with his students. However, both these episodes owed most of their importance to their other implications.

On December 4 L.S.E. Oration Day was again disrupted. Sir William Armstrong, head of the civil service, had come to address 600 graduates of L.S.E. Before this ceremony about 200 people, over half of them L.S.E. students, had held a meeting at which a motion was carried to the effect that six questions should be put to the governing body. The six questions were duly chanted. Lord Robbins ignored them. Two youths, neither from the L.S.E., mounted the platform and seized the microphone. Obscenities were shouted.

The following month the Oxford Union was disturbed. A debate on overseas aid was being held to mark the visit of an American debating team. 150 students, led by the Pakistani revolutionary, entered singing the 'Internationale'. They had come from a meeting organized to form an Oxford Solidarity Action Committee opposed to the projected visits of Herr Adolf von Thadden, the Right-wing German politician, and the Reverend Ian Paisley, the protestant leader in Northern Ireland.

On the same day, January 22, 1970, it was announced that Mr. Powell had cancelled his planned visit to Dundee University. The university's Conservative Association alleged that publicly uttered threats by the Extreme Left had made it impossible to guarantee Mr. Powell's safety—particularly as the vice-chancellor, Mr. Drever, had publicized his unwillingness to have Mr. Powell or Herr von Thadden on university property. He had, the Association alleged, stated that no action would be taken against disrupters and had refused to admit the police to the campus.

In the same month some undergraduates of Oriel College, Oxford, disrupted a meeting of the college governing body and demanded that the proposed increase in the price of meals should be referred to the domestic committee. This was conceded. The following week a new code of rules made rustication or expulsion possible punishments for future disruptions. The increase had been proposed because there was a large deficit in the previous year's domestic account.

By now the Pakistani revolutionary had left Oxford and with 50 Black Power supporters occupied a former school in Manchester. Thus Oxford was not further disturbed, except by the Files Controversy, for the moment.

Also in January 1970 a Conservative Association meeting at

Goldsmith's College, London, was disrupted. Lieutenant-Colonel Cao Xuan Ve, of the South Vietnamese Embassy, was the target of bottles, beer glasses and toy bricks. The chairman of London University Conservative Association commented, 'Interruptions and comment are expected when controversial subjects are being discussed but this was violence and hooliganism. Those responsible should be severely dealt with.' He complained that Goldsmith's authorities were failing in their duty by not taking action against the eight or ten students responsible for the disruption.

Meanwhile firms with interests in South Africa and Rhodesia had ceased to hold recruiting interviews for L.S.E. students in L.S.E. itself. L.S.E. authorities had not pressed them to this display of caution, though the president of the students' union had requested the director to ask the interviewers to go elsewhere.

Mr. Powell spoke to Bradford University Tories without disturbance. The chairman of the Conservative Association said, 'We kept the meeting as secret as possible and arranged the way out for Mr. Powell with the library authorities and the police. He came in the same way.' He arranged that while police kept potential demonstrators out of view the audience extended its end-of-meeting applause. While they were clapping Mr. Powell was escorted from the second-floor meeting room at Bradford Central Library and down a goods lift to a loading bay, where a car was waiting.

February 1970 saw student onslaughts on three well-known Conservatives. At Kent University fireworks were used in the reception given to Mr. Heath, leader of the party. Sir Gerald Nabarro, M.P. for Worcestershire South, was shouted down at Hull when he opposed the legalization of cannabis. He insisted that there should be no repetition of this when he addressed students at Warwick University. But the most significant episode of this type to occur in February was the decision of Sussex University union council by 14 votes to 12 to refuse permission to the university's Conservative Association to invite Mr. Wall to address it in the university. The vice-chancellor refused to comment. He said that it was a students' union matter. There were precedents for this condoned exclusion. In the previous summer term Sir Archibald James had come to the university to speak on Rhodesia and had been prevented from entering by several hundred people. He had been advised by a university official to leave the premises.

March and April were, in this sense, quieter. Mr. Short, however, was disturbed when opening the new Oxford Polytechnic. The president of the students' union invited Mr. Short to take the microphone and answer criticisms of the plans for the new poly. Mr. Short refused and was booed. At L.S.E. a South Vietnamese representative was driven out with shouts and fireworks.

May was more eventful. Eldon Griffiths was noisily received at the Oxford Union. However, the chief figures were Mr. Ronald Bell, Conservative M.P. for South Buckinghamshire, and Mr. Michael Stewart, Foreign Secretary in the Labour government. Mr. Bell spoke at Leeds University at the invitation of the Conservative Association. During the first part of his speech there were cries of 'fascist pig!' and 'fascist slob!' emerging from a background of whistling, clapping and stamping. Mr. Bell went on to speak of immigration. Then, of the most active disrupters about 30 advanced on the platform. One mounted it. There were scuffles. Mr. Bell asked the meeting if it wished him to continue. Receiving no clear response he left the university and went to a nearby hotel. Meanwhile one of the disrupters stood on a chair and said, 'Ronald Bell is a consistent supporter of the racialists in this country and abroad; he is anti-trade union, and he is opposed to equal pay for women.'

The reception given to Mr. Stewart at the Oxford Union was as noisy and, because of Mr. Stewart's position, possibly more important. Mr. Stewart was the main speaker against the motion, 'That this house has no confidence in Her Majesty's Government's foreign policy'. 100 students booed, jeered, whistled and threw paper pellets. There were cries of 'Resign, you bum', 'Stewart, we want you dead', 'Murderer, murderer. Sharpeville, Pinkville' and 'Ho Chi Minh'. A noose was hung from the gallery just behind his head. He was jostled as, abandoning his attempt to speak, he left the Union under police escort. The doors were slammed to keep the students in. Mr. Stewart said, 'I should think twice before coming again. If this was a country in a revolutionary situation, this sort of behaviour could be understood.'

The following week Oxford Union voted overwhelmingly for the condemnation of this disruption. This motion was proposed by

Mr. Stephen Milligan, president of the Union and chairman of the Conservative Association, and opposed by the leader of the Socialist Society who had proposed the motion of no confidence the previous week.

33 of the disrupters were identified. Only 13 of them were members of the Union. Mr. Milligan wished to have them expelled from the Union if they did not apologize to Mr. Stewart. Mr. Stewart wrote to the Union saying that he realized that the disrupters were in a minority. Mr. Hugh Fraser, Conservative M.P. for Stafford and Stone, who was to have spoken the previous week, wrote to say that he would be happy to return and speak in the Union.

June 1970 saw the year's last suppression of differing opinions. Mr. Julian Amery, candidate for Brighton Pavilion, visited Sussex University to speak on 'Conservative Victory'. When he described Chairman Mao Tse Tung as a 'butcher and a mass murderer', there was a barrage of eggs, flour and crockery and an attempt to disconnect the microphone. Mr. Amery left the hall, pursued by 60 Maoists in a crowd of about 150 people. Some of the Maoists carried banners and chanted 'Racists out'. Mr. Amery's speech was later broadcast over the university's closed circuit television system. The vice-chancellor said that students were 'foolish' in the middle of an election campaign not to allow candidates of whatever party to put their case, however unpalatable a speaker's views might be. The 'Students for a Labour Victory' group blamed 'ultra Left-wing' demonstrators for the disruption which they did not support.

The years 1968–70 saw the acceptance of disruption as endemic and progressive. Academic, social and political life was interfered with at all levels. Mr. Powell could not be invited to a Cambridge Ball and Professor Day could not give his lectures. The erosion of the security of expression of opinion had taken hold.

Thus these two years continued and developed the disturbances at art colleges and the attack on freedom of speech in institutions of higher and further education.

4

Games, Files and Trials

THE ACADEMIC year 1969–70 followed the pattern of its predecessor. The targets of attack, however, changed. Vietnam receded from the consciousness of restive students and was replaced by South Africa. Within the universities the occasion for disturbance changed from student power to student files. Both episodes showed the extension of student claims to special consideration.

The year started quietly. Expansion of numbers was continuing to be a problem. On October 1 Sir Eric Ashby, vice-chancellor of Cambridge, asserted that further growth in student numbers was likely to be accommodated in smaller new universities. On October 6 the Federation of Conservative Students published its Students' Charter. This, although uncompromising on the necessity of discipline for disrupters, defended non-obstructive sit-ins. On the same day Mr. Jack Straw of the N.U.S. claimed that the vice-chancellors had conceded student representation on committees for the sake of peace. 'The universities, by making concessions on this basis, have purchased not time but a time-bomb.' However, he did not think that students should elect staff or decide what should be taught. He did not want control through mass meetings. It was not entirely clear what he wanted. The next day the second Black Paper came out and brought frankly expressed comments from both admirers and detractors.

L.S.E. governors offered increased student representation on committees. This was refused by the students' union. At Lancaster two students were fined for drug offences by a court composed of six students and six staff. The Cambridge Union condemned the government by 417 votes to 315; the previous year it had carried the same motion by 493 to 295. The mid-October demonstrations in support of the American War Moratorium were poorly supported. 300 demonstrated in Grosvenor Square. In L.S.E., as already stated, audiences could only be obtained for speakers supporting the Moratorium by holding meetings in the bar. The report of the select committee investigating student unrest was published; it deplored the control of union policy by mass meetings.

This calm did not survive the first half of October. On the 16th the Oxford Union voted to support the protest planned against the visit of the Springboks, the all-white South African rugby team, to Oxford where they were to play the Oxford University rugby team. This was an omen of what was to come.

On the same day about 100 students locked the governors in a room of the Enfield College of Technology. The staff and students were demonstrating in support of their demand for a meeting to discuss allegations of mismanagement of college funds. It was an unfortunate choice of day for the announcement that education expansion might result in increased taxation.

The Springboks visit began to assume greater importance. It both polarized and confused opinion. Some approved of the South African government and wished to welcome its team on those grounds; these were in a minority. Some disapproved strongly of the South African government and of its rugby team's playing against British sides, and were prepared to translate this disapproval into the forcible prevention of matches; these, too, were in a minority. In between were those who disapproved both of the matches and of the prospect of violence, in varying proportions. On October 19 Mr. Dennis Howell, Minister of Sport, spoke for one section of the last-named group when he said, 'I do not think the South African team should come—I have no time for any sport based on racial considerations.' More determined opposition was being organized by the vice-chairman of the Young Liberals, a student at Imperial College, London.

On October 21 there was a demonstration at Senate House, London University. 30 or 40 people were involved in a disturbance occasioned by their protest against London University's links with the University College of Rhodesia. One of those leading the protest was an American revolutionary student registered at

Bedford College, London. He had already been ordered by a court of law to keep away from the L.S.E. where he had been a prominent figure in the disturbances of 1968–69. On October 27 1,000 students, mostly from University College, London, demonstrated outside Senate House because they felt that in the previous week's demonstration excessive force had been used by the staff. The students invited Sir Douglas Logan, the principal of London University, to come out and talk to them. He declined this invitation and the president of University College students' union went in to see him. This concession caused some of the Extreme Left to jeer at the president.

Meanwhile students at other institutions had not been idle. On October 23 St. Andrews University students' representative council declared void the decision of a student meeting which had voted by 151 to 110 in favour of sending the rector, Sir Learie Constantine, a letter demanding his resignation on grounds of ill-health. Some of his attitudes had displeased them. There were over 2,000 students at St. Andrews. The rector did not resign.

By October 24 the tension aroused by the projected visit of the Springboks to Oxford became such that the venue was changed. 'Oxford, reject apartheid' had been blazoned on the grass of the pitch. Developments at Cambridge were less destructive materially; there the Socialist Society, which had absorbed and replaced the Labour Club, formed a Philby Club in honour of the well-known Soviet agent.

On October 30 the Springboks came to Britain. They were met by about 20 hostile Reading University students as well as the official reception committee. The most publicized student activity of the year was about to begin.

On November 1 it was announced that an Oxford University committee set up to study discipline was to adopt some of the Hart recommendations and pass them on to the Hebdomadal Council which has much of the control of the university in its hands. Students were to be represented on disciplinary boards. They were to have the right of appeal before being sent down or rusticated for more than a term. Senior as well as junior members of the university were to be subject to discipline, although in their case it would be decided by a board set up by the university's Visitor. Occupations, disruption of work and damage to university property were all to be statutory offences. Proctors, tutors with disciplinary powers, were to keep them. The effectiveness of a compromise could be seen later in the year.

At Enfield College of Technology activist staff and students were together opposing the governors. The lock-in had been succeeded by the declaration by the academic board to the Council for National Academic Awards that it could no longer guarantee 'the competent academic operation' of the institution. Staff and students had broken off their newly acquired representation on the governing body. Students had on October 31 picketed a meeting of a committee of the governing body. This particular conflict had begun in July with the decision of the chairman of the governors, Councillor Barry Lewis, to exclude the newly elected college members of the governing body from a meeting. In its letter to the C.N.A.A. the academic board now alleged that proposals brought by the governing body contained clauses discriminating against staff and students and rejected college proposals for the reorganization of the arts faculty. As a result of this letter the chairman of the governing body sent a message to the staff and students without consulting the principal first.

Division over the Springboks sharpened. Oxford Firework Committee declared its intention of protesting at the Oxford-Springboks match, while Eastbourne town council voted 19 to 10 in favour of entertaining the South African team.

Leaflets were distributed at the Springboks' hotel. Coaches were ordered to take demonstrators to Twickenham where the match was to be played. A spokesman for the Anti-Apartheid Group said, 'We are not committed to a disruptive form of protest.' The Young Liberal leader of the Anti-Springboks Group was firmer. The view of the Oxford rugby team was expressed by its captain: 'We have never wavered in our intention to play the game. Contrary to the expressed opinion of the Firework Committee we are not hiding behind the Rugby Football Union. We are simply fulfilling a public responsibility in removing the game from Oxford. In some respects I feel a certain sympathy with the cause, but the fact remains that the right to play the game, which we intend to do, is exclusively ours.' However, the Twickenham game's demonstrations on November 5 were less disruptive than had been hoped and feared. One demonstrator commented, 'We only had twelve hours

to prepare for this. We shall be much better organized at Leicester.'
This was the venue of the next match. Leicester police shared their
expectations and asked for the help of London and Midlands police
forces. However, although there was trouble, the match was played
to its conclusion and it began to seem that despite the efforts of the
Anti-Springboks Group the tour would not be disrupted.

Meanwhile normal internal university disturbances continued.
During the summer 4 Essex students had been suspended on
academic and other grounds. As a result of this early in November
about 100 students barricaded a meeting of Essex Senate and locked
it in, thus following the precedent set by Enfield. Then they intercepted a letter sent by a university proctor asking members of the
senate to identify the blockading students and described this as
victimization. On November 6 an Essex students' union meeting
attended by 400 people demanded an independent public enquiry
into staff-student relations within the university and resolved to
petition the Department of Education and Science for such an
enquiry. The meeting set a deadline for the Senate to confirm this
decision. However this policy was the following day repudiated
by the union's executive council which declared that the resolution
to petition the Department of Education and Science was ill-
conceived, that such a petition would not serve the interests of the
four students suspended, would endanger academic standards,
would imperil the existence of Essex as an independent university
and would be of no use in solving internal problems. The council
also regretted both the blockade of the senate and its execution in
defiance of the decision of an earlier student meeting. However, on
November 10 a three-hour union meeting attracted 700 students,
carried a motion of no confidence in the university authorities,
voted to ask the Department of Education and Science for a public
enquiry into assessment procedures, decided that an internal
enquiry should be held the following week, all classes being
suspended, and resolved that in the event of there being no public
enquiry Lord Gifford should be approached to hold one at the
union's expense. After this meeting excitement sank somewhat.

There were other normal conflicts at other institutions. The
expulsion of a pregnant student from Hamilton College of Education brought about the resignation of the students' union
representative council and the involvement of the Scottish Union

of Students. In London the entire executive of the central council of Bar students resigned in order to leave the field clear for the militants. On November 11 a meeting attracted 400 of the 1,400 law students of the Inns of Court and made far-reaching demands for representation on decision-making bodies. An action committee of 17 was elected. One member said, 'We hope, now that we have a new and far more militant action committee, that we will achieve our demands. They have become urgent and imperative.'

The Springboks continued to provide the main outlet for the energies of activist students. On November 10 the Young Liberal leader said, 'Swansea is going to be a very important game for us. We have not actually stopped a match yet; in the face of police opposition we have done everything but that and we are hoping to succeed at Swansea. If not, at one of the two matches immediately after.' Swansea University College prepared for the day; its union condemned the match and made night facilities available to students from London, Oxford, Sussex, Cardiff, Aberystwyth and Newport.

The following day the motion 'Political commitment should not intrude upon sporting contacts' was debated by Cambridge Union. It was lost by 344 votes to 160. Mr. Dennis Howell, Minister of Sport, was the chief speaker against the motion and Mr. Edward Dexter, the well-known cricketer, was the chief speaker for it. Apprehension was spreading. Some Aberdeen councillors were alarmed by the possibility of violence at the Springboks match due to be played in the city. At Newport there was a torchlight procession on November 11 by 150 people. However, the game the next day passed off peacefully.

On November 16 the long-awaited Swansea match took place. There were 1,500 demonstrators of whom seven were hurt and 67 arrested and 1,000 policemen of whom ten were hurt. There were also 200 vigilantes. As a result of the conflicts at this match Swansea students' union demanded an enquiry into responsibility for it. The Young Liberal leader said, 'Demonstrators are so annoyed about the action of the vigilantes in particular that Ebbw Vale could make Swansea seem like a teaparty.'

Two minor episodes at this time are of interest. On November 18 a new course, Human Sciences, was approved by 153 to 122 by

Oxford Congregation; in view of the narrowness of the vote the question was remitted to a postal vote. Also on November 18 a referendum was held by Cambridge Union to decide whether to admit to membership students from Cambridge Technical College and students from abroad working in the city but not registered at university colleges. The referendum resulted in the overwhelming rejection of the proposal of extension of membership. This decision was denounced as 'stupid, selfish and squalid' by the president, Mr. Hugh Anderson. Thus tradition and inequality seemed to retain their hold in matters immediately affecting staff and students.

On November 19 the Ebbw Vale match was held. There were 15,000 spectators, 420 policemen and 200 demonstrators. The match was quiet. The Young Liberal leader's fears had proved groundless.

Attempts were made to damage pitches. At Aldershot glass was scattered on the ground. This provided a precedent followed when opposition to the South African cricket tour was organized. However, determination to carry on with the Springboks matches remained firm. The North District Rugby Union threatened to oppose legally any action by Aberdeen Corporation that might lead to the cancellation of the Rugby Union's lease of the Corporation's ground for the match. On the same day, November 20, a further occasion for bitterness was provided by the complaint to the Race Relations Board that a South Coast doctor had advertised for a Scottish cook.

On November 21 the N.U.S. autumn conference met at Margate. It passed a resolution opposing the institution of computer records on students for statistical reasons. It voted that no educational institution should keep records of students' political or religious beliefs without their consent and that students should have the right to see transcripts of their records and evaluations of conduct. It also carried the usual proposal for a review of grants. At this last meeting fewer than 400 of the 1,000 delegates were present. The conference also condemned the use of violence to disrupt the Springbok tour.

Discussions continued unaffected by these deliberations. On November 24 by 175 to 6 votes Inns of Court students decided to sit-in. They held a sing-song. Not all the 175 students who voted for it joined the occupation. On November 25 the fear of violence at the Springboks match planned for Ulster became so great that the game was cancelled. On November 26 a Springboks match was played in Manchester. There were 2,000 police and 7,000 demonstrators of whom some carried bicycle chains. There were 150 arrests. The president of Manchester students' union said that he had received twenty complaints of police behaviour but 'in the main the police were fairly good'. The cost to the Lancashire ratepayers was £7,500.

However some disagreements were relatively peaceful. On November 24 the Cambridge Union carried an emergency motion calling for the cancellation of any university hockey, squash or tennis matches against South African teams. On November 28 the electoral contest for the presidency of the Oxford Union attracted fewer than 400 voters.

Plans were made to disrupt the Springboks match scheduled for Eire. The Irish Congress of Trade Unions instructed its members not to provide the Springboks with any services. There were sit-downs in front of the Dublin offices of the Irish Rugby Football Union. At Aberdeen the Chief Constable was apprehensive. The Springboks match played there on December 2 justified his view. There were 98 arrests. A policeman's shoulder was broken. Before the match two M.P.s and some councillors had held a silent vigil near the ground despite the Chief Constable's reminder that in other places 'such dignified expressions of dissent' had been used to conceal the actions of 'evilly intentioned persons whose object is violence'.

On December 1 a large majority of the Cambridge University consultative committee had approved a motion 'regretting that teams representing the university should play against teams selected on racial grounds'. This seemed a belated discovery and expression of opinion. Both moderate and extreme, non-violent and violent, opposition to games against South African teams was growing in universities.

The problem of the expansion of student numbers was attracting attention again. In order to deal with the consequences of the post-war rise in the birth-rate the government made on December 3 thirteen suggestions for accommodating the extra students in view. These were: the reduction or removal of student grants, coupled with a system of loans; a similar policy at post-graduate level only; a more restrictive policy on the admission of overseas students; a requirement that grant-aided students should enter specified kinds of employment for a period after graduation; a greater use of part-time and correspondence courses as alternatives to full-time study; the compression of courses to two years for able students; the institution of a two-year sub-degree course; the insertion of a period of time between leaving school and going to university; the more intensive use of buildings and equipment coupled with the reorganization of the academic year; the sharing of facilities among various institutions; the increase of the proportion of students living at home and attending local universities; the development of student housing associations and other forms of loan-financed provision for student residence, and a change in the staff-student ratio. These proposals were, except for one, attacked by the committee of vice-chancellors. In a letter to the University Grants Committee the vice-chancellors wrote, 'The contribution which universities wish to make over the years to 1982, is first, to provide, over a wide range of subjects, education and professional training in no way inferior to the quality being given today, second, to offer education to a proportion of the age-group at least as well-qualified to receive it as the students being admitted today; and, third, to maintain, by research done by university teachers, the substantial contribution which British universities make to the advancement of knowledge.' On the proposals the Association of University Teachers commented, in opposing all the suggestions except that of sharing facilities, that the proportion of government expenditure on the universities could well rise from 0.65 to 1 per cent. This episode showed clearly the extent of the problem of the growth in the numbers of young people and the desperation and inconsistency of the methods suggested for coping with it. It must be viewed in conjunction with London University's warning later in the month that the number of graduates was now such that graduates were having to take jobs previously considered beneath them.

Meanwhile the South African controversy continued. 100 Labour and Liberal M.P.s signed a letter on December 4 to the effect that if an exclusively white South African cricket team came in 1970 they would join the protests. The Irish Post Office

Officials' Union decided to stop work during the Springboks game in Eire. The Senior Treasurer's Committee of Oxford University decided that any university sports team playing against a racially selected team would be refused a grant from the central grants fund. The Labour Chancellor of the Duchy of Lancaster, Mr. George Thomson, warned, 'My generation regarded the doctrine of violence as the hall-mark of fascism and as the Second World War approached took to violence rationally and reluctantly as the lesser evil—the only way to defeat fascism and preserve a tolerant and humane society and the possibility of peaceful social and economic change.' The Conservative former leader of Newcastle city council took a more drastic line and suggested arming civilians to help the police.

There were some speeches of slight interest made on related topics at this time. Mr. Jack Straw alleged on December 9 that Nottingham students were being denied electoral representation. In fact, it was his general contention that Conservative party agents were trying to deprive students of their right to vote in their university towns. The vice-chancellor of Lancaster, Sir Charles Carter, claimed on December 10 that modern students were not idle. The most important and ominous pronouncement was made by Sir William Mansfield-Cooper, vice-chancellor of Manchester University. He had been concerned about a wave of unrest at Manchester. 400 students had held a brief sit-in at Whitworth Hall, an administration block. They had been protesting about the selection of a successor to Sir William without student consultation. On December 10 Sir William said, 'I am sure there will be a move to bring in specific penalties. I am gathering information about these protesters and am accumulating my findings . . . I believe that many of these agitators are not university students at all but people from outside.' This speech was later used to give substance to the allegations made in the Files Controversy.

Tension in the South African dispute did not slacken. A Springboks match planned for a Bournemouth ground had to have its name changed because it was a difficult venue for the police to defend. On the same day, December 11, the Test and County Cricket Board unanimously decided to invite the South African cricket team for the following year.

On December 12 Lord Bowden, principal of the University of Manchester Institute of Science and Technology, said that there was no necessity to place in universities all those technically qualified to attend. This view was denounced by many, including some of his students.

On December 16 the South African authorities announced that their next year's cricket team would be entirely white. This increased feeling, which had on the same day been less violently articulated at the Springboks match at Aldershot. There were only 170 demonstrators, including a large contingent from nearby Surrey University, and they were herded into a special demonstrators' arena, away from the 5,000 rugby fans. On December 19 the Young Liberal leader expressed his hopes for the match to be played at Twickenham. 'We are expecting between 5,000 and 10,000 demonstrators headed by the Bishop of Woolwich.' In the event fewer demonstrators arrived but they were energetic. A police-station was invaded.

The Irish Rugby Union refused to cancel its arrangements with the Springboks. Kent County Cricket Council declared its intention of playing the South African cricket team and thereupon received some resignations and many offers of help. On this note of assertiveness on both sides 1969 ended. It must be remembered that all these events took place in a general climate of youthful indifference. As in the previous year there were complaints about the difficulty of persuading the newly-enfranchised young to bother to register for the vote. On December 27 Conservative Central Office estimated that only 60 per cent of 18-to-21-year-olds were registered.

1970 began with the knighting of Dr. Walter Adams, the Director of L.S.E., and the binding over for a year of an Essex University Young Liberal for putting a smoke-bomb in a Bristol hotel where the Springboks were staying.

However the results of past activities were less interesting than the expectation of new excitement. On January 5 there was a 300-strong Anti-Apartheid Group march in Coventry to protest against the Springboks match to be held there. On January 6 the match was held. There were 1,100 police and 1,500 demonstrators. The following day the Springboks arrived in Dublin. They ignored some 50 people sitting down and throwing eggs. A man was charged with possessing explosives outside the Springboks' hotel. By now the impetus behind the Anti-Springboks movement seemed to have slowed for the time being. When the Springboks played at Galashiels on January 16 there were 20 demonstrators and 400 police.

This did not indicate that Scottish universities were quiet. On an intellectual level Edinburgh activists published in January 1970 'The Red Paper' as a reply to the Black Paper. On a more direct level some students staged a sit-in in the university's appointment offices in 'protest against racialism and the university's tacit support of firms with direct economic interests in South Africa'. While there the students broke open the confidential files and published some of their contents. It is of interest that the only 'incriminating' comment they could find was that one student might be a Jew. The students' representative council which had not decreed the sit-in, demanded an enquiry into the appointments service. The Conservative Association of the university asserted that the authorities had failed in their duty by allowing the students responsible for the break-in 'to continue unhindered'. It stated: 'Society must not tolerate behaviour which reflects the law of the jungle and allows gross invasions of privacy and a situation which allows a minority to get away with holding society itself to ransom. . . . the university has also failed to establish its faith in the rule of law . . . It also leads that group to suppose that they will be able to repeat their vandalism.' This series of events was destined to be repeated in several British universities.

A different source of disturbance made itself felt among Welsh students. On January 15, 50 students barricaded themselves into the court-room of the Shire Hall, Carmarthen. They were protesting against the gaol sentence just passed on Mr. Dafydd Ewan, chairman of the Welsh Language Society. Mr. Ewan had been sentenced for refusing to pay a £56 fine for daubing over road signs in English. The students sang Welsh songs and announced that they would sit-in until noon, thus preventing the quarter-sessions from sitting. Meanwhile in Aberystwyth 27 students sat down for an all-night occupation in a court-room there.

Ireland, too, had its academic troubles that month. The students' representative council at Queen's University, Belfast, demanded one-third student representation on all academic committees and that staff-student departmental committees should be given some executive and administrative power.

However there was more disturbance in the capital than anywhere else. On January 13 there was a struggle between police and Extreme Left wing students outside L.S.E. The students, about 200 of them, had been protesting about the selection of a new vice-chairman of the governors without students being consulted. On January 17 a slightly more moderate group of London postgraduate students made an attempt to persuade Convocation, the policy-making association of London University graduates, to elect them to its standing committee. However, although this graduate group canvassed all the colleges of London, its members obtained only about 100 votes each and were defeated. They said that they would try for election to London University senate the following May but later they abandoned this plan. On January 25 there was a Vietnam demonstration in Whitehall. There was a struggle between the 2,000 demonstrators and the police. The marchers were led by the Pakistani revolutionary.

More mundane matters agitated some institutions. At Brunel University 500 students boycotted the refectory in protest at rises in the prices of meals. This tendency was more marked in the provinces. At York, where the student newspaper *Nouse* had recently been taken over by the Extreme Left, some students were supporting gipsy demands opposed by the local council, for a permanent site and were teaching gipsy children on the campus. One type of discrimination continued to prevail there; it was the women students who looked after the children while the men students distributed the leaflets. At Hull University the president of the students' union, who had been elected on the platform 'Vote academic thug!', resigned because the union executive elected more recently objected to his not consulting the authorities concerned in his planning of a merger of room facilities with the College of Education next door. The president had, the previous November, complained that Hull University students did not take enough interest in 'wider educational issues'. At Bolton 300 students held a two-hour sit-in in the town hall in protest against a corporation decision to end full-time G.C.E. courses at technical colleges for people under 19. This had been proposed to relieve pressure on money and space.

The following month saw the Files Controversy develop. On February 3 after a students' union meeting attended by about 400 people, 300 Warwick students held an occupation of the university registry in support of their demand for a totally-integrated staff-student social amenities building jointly controlled by the users. The 9 members of the sit-in-committee were threatened with disciplinary action but the matter was dropped. On February 11 another 300-strong sit-in was held with the support of the students' union. The president promised the authorities that there would be no damage. The files were broken open and 'incriminating' documents copied. The most incriminating of these documents were two letters sent by people outside the university to the vice-chancellor on the activities of former lecturers and the rejection of a candidate for entrance who had been a member of the Schools Action Union. There was no evidence that the university had taken any notice of the information offered on its lecturers. There was every indication that the information on the candidate's membership of the S.A.U. had not been offered as a warning. The rest of the reference was glowing. Warwick was the candidate's last choice of university, and he had been accepted by Sussex, the university of his first choice. On these foundations a whole edifice of suspicion was built.

Meanwhile other causes of disturbance had made themselves felt. Cricket-pitches intended for the South African Tour's use had been dug up. Some of the leaders of the Young Liberals shared the responsibility for this.

Welsh nationalism voiced itself again. On February 4 14 students from the University College of Aberystwyth disrupted the hearing of a libel case in London. They were gaoled for three months. However, although they refused to apologize, they were released the following week. The principal of their college made his view clear. 'The senate completely dissociates itself from the demonstration. The students who took part in it absented themselves without asking for leave and this aspect is now being dealt with through the disciplinary procedure of the college.' This disruption had been accompanied by the singing of 'We shall overcome' in Welsh. In the event 20 Welsh Justices of the Peace helped Mr. Ewan to pay the fine which had led to this series of disturbances.

However Warwick soon reasserted its claims to primacy in these matters. On February 12 a large meeting was held to discuss the newly taken documents. The vice-chancellor obtained an injunction to prevent publication. On February 13 over 1,000 staff and students attended another meeting. The students held two meetings that day. A committee of seven was appointed by one of these. The staff held a meeting attended by over half their number. This demanded the 'immediate destruction' of all political documents on staff. By 65 votes to 34 with 19 abstentions the staff demanded the strong discouragement of the sending of such documents from people outside the university. However, they were unanimous in passing a resolution extending 'goodwill' to all involved in the disputes.

A different type of disturbance now arose in Cambridge. Its only recent contribution to student turmoil had been on February 9 when 50 students occupied an empty house in order to turn it into a refuge for alcoholics. On February 13 this precedent of the extension of student rights over non-university property was followed. A Greek Banquet held at the Garden House Hotel was disturbed by 400 students. At least £1,000 worth of damage was done and several policemen and a proctor were injured. It was claimed by the Left that this was an appropriate reaction to the condonation of the Greek government implied by the holding of the Banquet. Several students were charged in connection with this riot. Oxford, on the other hand, was as yet quiet. Its only claim to attention was its refusal by a vote of 183 to 101 of Congregation to raise fees for overseas students.

A local target for student protest appeared at Swansea University College. 15 students at a hall of residence refused to accept the regulations of their hostel. These regulations were being examined by the university. The seven members of the students' union executive council became involved in the dispute. All 22 were suspended. 2,300 of the 3,000 students of the college went on strike. They were supported by the N.U.S. An independent enquiry was demanded. 100 staff signed a statement expressing sympathy with the students. The strike lasted and achieved its purpose. The authorities said that the 15 from the hostel 'may have believed that they were being asked to sign away, under duress, some of their rights as citizens of a free and civilized country'.

An omen for the future was provided at Edinburgh in February.

The principal of the university declared his intention of disciplining those involved in the previous month's break-in. He alleged that some of the culprits were not members of the university. The protesters claimed that a petition they had organized urging reform of the appointments service, and asserting a students' right to see any files containing information on himself, had obtained 700 signatures.

Warwick students had demanded an independent enquiry. The senate, having condemned the occupation and the break-in, agreed to the proposed enquiry under Lord Radcliffe, the chancellor of the institution. However it ignored the students' demand for the suspension of the vice-chancellor during the enquiry. The enquiry duly began though the students did not, as they had wished, share in running it.

Demands for enquiries were not confined to the Left. At East Anglia two students asked for an enquiry to be held into the alleged misuse of students' union funds. They said, 'These funds, provided chiefly by the local education authorities, are intended to provide amenities for students. They should not be used to pay the fines of students who break the law of the land or to make contributions to liberation movements in Southern Africa.' The president of the East Anglian union denied that any such misuse had occurred at East Anglia, although some of the profits from union dances had been paid to the Peoples' Democracy Movement of Ireland. This demand indicated a concern, which events were to show well-grounded, that union meetings would influence not only official union policy but also, by implication and then directly, the policies and purses of individual political associations within the student body.

Such wide issues indeed agitated several student bodies at this time. Essex was the best-known case. On February 17 a student meeting unanimously condemned South Africa, Rhodesia and Portugal for their apartheid policies, asserted that Barclays Bank was supporting these regimes and enjoined the university and all within it to sever all connection with the Bank. The leaders of this campaign said they had collected several hundred signatures supporting it and planned a mass withdrawal on February 19. On that day 100 students stormed the campus branch of Barclays and put two students, symbolizing Barclays Bank and university

4

investments, on the counter. The bank took on extra staff to deal with the expected wave of withdrawals but there were only 60. However more drastic attempts were planned by some. Three students were arrested for trying to burn the bank down. King's College, Cambridge, was more restrained. By a large majority a students' union meeting called on the college council to withdraw all remaining investments in South Africa, to close the college's account with Barclays and transfer them to the Co-operative Bank. However Cambridge as a whole remained undisturbed by the Barclays Controversy and by the Files Controversy. The senate of the university had just vigorously condemned the Garden House Hotel riot, in connection with which legal proceedings were now being organized.

The Files Controversy was now spreading. At York a large students' meeting demanded that every student should, within two hours of the meeting, be given permission to see the file on him. Lord James, the vice-chancellor, maintained that the files should be 'absolutely confidential'. The authorities' proposal that the local M.P., Mr. Alex Lyon, should examine them for incriminating references to political belief was refused. However, the threat of 'direct action' was not then carried out. Eventually an agreement to discuss 'non-confidential material' was reached. The Warwick letters had been printed and distributed anonymously at York. The university students' newspaper had advertised them without indicating their contents. Thus it avoided legal action. Lancaster students also published the Warwick letters.

At Oxford there was on February 24 an occupation by about 400 of administrative buildings. The plan had its origin at Balliol. Attempts were made by a minority of sitters-in to take confidential files. The vice-chancellor of Lancaster denied that his university kept political files. So did the vice-chancellor of Manchester University. He refused to allow 'student invigilators' to examine his dossiers, asserting, 'There is nothing political in my dossiers.' On February 25 he obtained an injunction to prevent five of his students from organizing an occupation. Not only the University but the University of Manchester Institute of Science and Technology was affected. Its students' union demanded an independent enquiry into the Institute keeping secret files on students. The principal, Lord Bowden, offered to open the files to a Queen's Counsel. At U.M.I.S.T. trouble was small in scale. Only 30 were involved in a raid on the registrar's office. Of these only 3 were charged. At the University itself the sit-in once begun became very large-scale indeed. By the 26th there were 1,000 involved, led by a committee of 10. The union's proposal for an enquiry to their liking had been refused by the senate. On February 27, 3,000 people attended a union meeting. 500 slept in the university. On this day the committee of vice-chancellors condemned the keeping of political files. This did not influence the course of events.

At Southampton an occupation already begun continued. Some damage was done in an effort to gain access to files. This sit-in was supported by about 200. It issued a statement: 'We are under no illusion that Warwick University is an exceptional case. There are secret political files of students at Southampton. We demand the destruction of these files.' It also alleged that the university had 'an interlocking relationship' with the Ministry of Defence and the U.S.A.F. No evidence was offered for these assertions. Mr. Straw had suggested that the Warwick letters might be the tip of the iceberg. Many assumed its existence.

100 Aston students threatened a sit-in. At Leeds after some negotiation the university offered to allow individual students to inspect their own files—apart from those marked confidential. At the North-West Polytechnic, London, a students' union meeting threatened to occupy the college on March 12 unless the students could see their files. At Sussex a raid on the administration block was threatened. At Glasgow a deputation of students asked the university to open its student files. The most interesting events occurred at Reading where there were two separate and simultaneous series of demands. One resolution carried by a students' union meeting described the appointment of Lord Sherfield as Chancellor as 'not particularly diplomatic'. Lord Sherfield had advocated continuing trade with South Africa. The proposer of this motion of criticism of and opposition to the prospective chancellor's installation was a founder-member of the Stop-the-Seventies-Tour group. On the same day students also demanded access to the files to see if any political ones were kept. The registrar said that there were no political files and that he was not going to let the students examine the other files.

Birmingham College of Commerce had met the demand for access to files without opposition and had duly opened the files to student representatives. The resulting joint statement was clear: 'The conclusion of the representatives was that there was no evidence of any attempt on the part of the college authorities to request, record or collate information pertaining to the political activities and beliefs of the staff and students.' Allegations that such records existed were 'regarded as a misunderstanding by the students in the light of such investigations'. It seemed that the students' march of protest had been wasted. At Birmingham University nearby the Files Controversy was largely ignored although there was later a token one-night sit-in by about 100. Before leaving for the night the administrative staff made sure that everything was firmly locked up.

During February there was a postscript to the 'urgent and imperative' demands of some of the students at the Inns of Court. 12 of them—fewer than the action committee of 17—held a one-day hunger-strike. In the heat of the Files Controversy it made little impression.

Thus February ended. The disputes about the files had remained unresolved. The absence of evidence, let alone proof, had not prevented the repetition of the claim that political files were being kept on students. No apologies had been offered in cases where larceny had yielded no evidence.

The beginning of the next month saw the continuation and extension of 'direct action'. At Oxford there were now 500 students in occupation. At Leeds there were discussions with the authorities and an action committee was quickly elected. The Manchester occupation continued in full force. It was visited and encouraged by Mr. Jack Straw who described the vice-chancellor as an extremist. On March 3 at a meeting of nearly 3,000 students it was decided to continue the occupation until student demands were met. However, the senate refused to agree to an enquiry of the type proposed by the students. At the same meeting a proposal for a strike was put and it obtained 68 per cent of the votes of those present. Since it had not obtained 75 per cent the plan was dropped.

By now there were 800 in occupation at Oxford. Another brief sit-in at Southampton had resulted in damage to cabinets but no discoveries of the sort expected. At Glasgow students were allowed to examine their files in the presence of the assistant registrar; few bothered. More interest was shown at Edinburgh where a students' meeting declared that 55 students fined for January's break-in need not pay their fines. In order to prevent these fines being paid from union funds the Conservative Association successfully invoked the law.

York remained agitated. A student meeting refused to accept inspection of the files by any third party and an occupation started. At Newcastle it was proposed by the authorities that a solicitor should examine the files. At Sheffield the Extreme Left threatened to occupy the registrar's office if students were refused the right to look at their files. The vice-chancellor held a discussion with students and the matter was referred to the senate. At Bedford College, London, 300 students held a brief occupation and alleged that they had found political material in the files. The following day this claim was tacitly dropped. Although Bedford is chiefly a women's college the chairman of the occupation committee was a man. At Stirling University the students' representative council said that there would be an occupation of the administration block if 50 students would support it. 30 Dundee students sat in as a protest against the fines imposed at Edinburgh. At the Regent Street Polytechnic, London, 100 students demanded to see their files. The principal refused and was given a week to reconsider. A five-hour students' meeting at Liverpool University rejected a proposal for immediate occupation. At Strathclyde 200 students began to sit-in. Within half an hour students began to leave. The students' council held negotiations with the registrar.

Thus the first week of March witnessed widespread and virtually simultaneous disturbances. Most were on a small scale. Two were not. One took place at Kent University, Canterbury, where 800 students of the 2,000 at the institution were present at the beginning of an occupation. 200 of the staff opposed this sit-in and some refused to sign references until it stopped. The other disturbances took place at Nottingham University where 1,000 students were in occupation. On March 10 a student meeting was attended by 3,000 people and proposals to allow restricted access to some personal files were considered. The sit-in ended almost at once.

Meanwhile the Manchester occupation too was collapsing,

despite a message of support from Bradford University. Two of the students' council resigned. A march which was intended to attract at least 5,000 of the city's 20,000 students attracted 250 and when it returned to the university lost more than half those. The sit-in was effectively over by March 11.

However another had begun elsewhere. About 300 students occupied Liverpool administration block on March 9. Like the Reading ones before them they linked two sets of issues. In the first place they were protesting about political files and in the second they were demanding, by 246 to 15 with 36 abstentions according to a vote taken on March 10, the resignation of the chancellor, Lord Salisbury, because of his former presidency of the Anglo-Rhodesian Society. In vain an equal number of students marched round the administration block urging the occupants to come out. This occupation, the last of the well-publicized ones, did not have the support of a large proportion of students. The impetus of the Files Controversy was beginning to ebb.

At Sussex the senate and the students reached a compromise. Students were to have access to their personal files, but written permission had to be granted by the author of each document first. If this were refused the document would be destroyed. The planning committee stated that the university 'depended on the candour and integrity of relations between the faculty and students'. The 50 students who occupied the registry at University College, London, on March 10 had sunk to 20 the following day. At Imperial College, London, efforts had been confined to writing letters to the governors. Letters found at Leeds and Glasgow indicating the existence of political files and spying were proved to have been forged. At Keele student regret at a break-in in search of political files and spying was such that a collection was taken to pay for the damage and the president of the union apologized for the incident. However it was revealed that instructions had been found on how to deal with student unrest.

At one university disturbances took place which had nothing to do with either files or racialism. On March 11 a referendum was held at Exeter University on whether to take 'direct action' to have student visiting hours extended. The referendum's result was a rejection of 'direct action' by 589 to 339 votes. A ballot-box containing 214 voting slips was stolen by an Extreme Left-winger and thrown into the river. The president of the union informed the police. At a meeting later the same day the compromise sanctioned by the referendum was rejected by six votes. The president and five of the students' representative council resigned, alleging that the militants had 'consistently pointed a pistol' at them.

The Kent and Liverpool sit-ins wore on. At Liverpool the occupiers tried to mobilize the workers. This attempt failed. The local Conservative-controlled council condemned the sit-in and threatened the grants of local students involved; the Labour minority blamed the Conservatives for being repressive but made no positive suggestion. The local Labour M.P., Mr. Eric Heffer, said to the sitters-in, 'It is alienating those who are desperately trying to understand your problems; and you are unwittingly assisting all those who would impose harsh discipline on students and who would resort to reactionary means to deal with student problems . . . Your wise course now is to end the sit-in and work for your ideas through the students' union.' Unlike the Liverpool sit-in the Kent occupation suffered greatly from attrition. On March 13 there were 600. On March 18 there were 400. The occupation ended and the sitters-in left singing 'On and on and on'. When asked by the registrar 'Where to?' they returned no answer. After handing a letter to the registrar and singing the first verse of the 'Internationale' they dispersed. The Liverpool sit-in ended on March 20.

Warwick was now comparatively quiet. On March 17, however, there was a demonstration by about 100 students outside the Bishop of Coventry's house where the university council was meeting. They played musical instruments and hung an effigy of the vice-chancellor from a tree outside. They ignored complaints of noise from the student representatives outside.

On March 16 Lord Annan, vice-chancellor of University College, London, had delivered an address on the price of violence. Some down-payments on this were now being made. Liverpool University announced its intention of disciplining some of the disrupters. At Oxford five students were fined for their part in the occupation of the Clarendon administrative buildings. More serious charges, including assault on university officials, were to be made against another student. The National Union of Students announced its intention of establishing a fund to help students to fight legal actions.

It should be mentioned that local matters occupied some institutions still. Swansea College of Education followed the example of Swansea University College and had a mass boycott in support of freedom of choice of lodgings. At the University of Manchester Institute of Science and Technology, however, world problems were made the subject of a demonstration of about 80 students. At an honorary fellowship presentation they carried banners with the message 'No fellowships for weapons profiteers'. The demonstration and booing were directed against Mr. Sebastian de Ferranti, chairman of the Electrical and Electronics group. Thus commotions over matters unrelated to the mainstream of protest continued to ensure variety.

It is some measure of the way in which important university activities were obscured that the final approval of the rise in Oxford's fees for overseas students passed almost unnoticed amid the disturbances. This decision was made by postal vote of Congregation. Another change that was obscured was the decision of the Oxford Union Society, hitherto confined to private subscribers, to throw itself open to all students of the university. Financial difficulties were the reason.

March also saw the involvement of students with national politics. The Labour Party set up a Students for a Labour Victory group. Its leaders included Mr. Hugh Anderson, ex-president of the Cambridge Union, Mr. Trevor Fisk, ex-president of the N.U.S., and Mr. Straw, his successor. The youthful Liberals once more attracted attention also. The Young Liberal leader from Imperial College, London, indicated that the Stop-the-Seventy-Tour would extend its activities to indoor games played against white South African teams. Thus there was little chance that student activities would altogether die down.

April contained what can only be described as mopping-up operations. At Liverpool one student was expelled for using force on a university official and 9 were suspended. 30 students picketed the administration building in protest. 170 signed declarations that they were as responsible as the sentenced ten for the occupation. However after an exchange of letters with the registrar they took no action and did not leave the university to show solidarity with their colleagues. The students' representative council stated that while they had opposed the occupation they now wished to help their fellow-students. Nothing could be done until term started. The sentences had been announced in the vacation. When term started the Socialist Society tried to occupy the university's telephone exchange, but was prevented by porters. The official union representatives were less active. They adopted a proposal to ask the N.U.S. for a 'National Day of Action' by all students and staff at all universities on May 1. They also bestowed life membership of the students' union on the 10 punished students and any others who might be disciplined for their part in the sit-in. A week later on April 27 a students' union meeting attracted over 1,200 of the university's 6,000 students. It carried a proposal for a formal protest and a one-day strike. The president of the union criticized the punishments as 'excessive and savage'. He said, 'We are concerned about the local and national implications of these sentences. The ten did no damage. They went into Senate House and expressed a point of view.' He described the disciplinary tribunal as 'a kangaroo court'. One student said that the ten deserved a stiff sentence for their disruptive activities. He was shouted down. The Liverpool case attracted great interest. The N.U.S. deplored the sentences and said that it would fight 'tooth and nail' any attempt to discipline the other 170. A group of Conservative M.P.s congratulated Liverpool University authorities. A large number of Labour M.P.s and a large proportion of Liberal ones condemned the sentences as 'harsh under the circumstances'. There is no evidence that Liverpool University authorities were influenced by any of the reactions inside or outside the university.

In Essex, on April 15, 3 students were sent to Borstal for trying to burn down the Barclays Bank on the campus. One said, 'We only meant to do it for a cause.' The judge said, 'What you need, quite obviously, is to be taught discipline and the ordinary standards of civilized behaviour without which society cannot exist. This does not appear to be a subject within the curriculum of this university but this is what Borstal is for.' There was little reaction from the other students at first as the sentences were pronounced during the vacation. Earlier the students' representative council had tried to help the 3 students. When in February they had been released on bail the university had banned them from the campus, except for 100 yards of the front drive. The students' representative council had taken the matter to the High Court but it failed to secure the removal of the ban. The university's response to the judge's remarks now was to assert that Essex had a disciplinary system and was in any case a particularly quiet, law-abiding and hard-working university.

At Oxford a student was expelled because during the last occupation he had used force on a university official. In protest some students banged on the doors and windows of the house of the vice-chancellor, Mr. Alan Bullock. They later claimed that this was 'rough musicking' of the type once used by peasants to shame their oppressors. The expelled student addressed an audience of 100 and 60 occupied the University Chest, the financial headquarters of the university, before the police arrived and prevented any more from entering. On April 29 they claimed that in the University Chest they had found documents proving that Oxford University had shares in South African firms. This announcement had little impact on students, particularly as it was made in the vacation before examination term.

In London the American revolutionary student at Bedford was sent to prison for a month for disruptive activities at L.S.E. His imprisonment excited relatively little opposition. At a students' union meeting held on April 24 only 116 people voted for a proposal providing for direct action against the repression of students. On April 30 and May 1 there was an occupation. It was specifically described as a University of London rather than an L.S.E. occupation. At one point in it there were 13 people present in the Old Theatre, where sit-ins were always centred. The indifference of most of L.S.E. and other London University students compelled the revolutionaries to 'guerrilla warfare'. Some maps in the geography department were set on fire and an attempt was made to start a fire on the library roof.

At Keele seven students appeared before a disciplinary committee for their part in the files break-ins. Three were suspended. This was condemned as 'a mockery of justice' by a student meeting which, however, took no action.

At Kent the university authorities wrote on April 15 letters to all students warning them that further direct action might bring expulsions. They claimed that the sitters-in of the previous term had been guilty of 'monstrous theft to the extent of £500, that damage done had cost £800 and that other costs had come to £1,500'. Like Kent authorities the Nottingham ones did not directly punish for past offences. They asked, also on April 15, some leaders of the sit-in to sign documents undertaking to instigate no more acts of disruption. The vice-chancellor, Professor Dainton, wrote, 'Sit-ins are always unlawful and irregular, no matter how great the efforts to keep them non-violent or to minimize damage.' At first the students refused categorically. Then one signed. Three professed themselves willing to sign on certain conditions, including that it would not be used against them in any subsequent disciplinary proceedings. Five still refused entirely. Their leader said, 'We will sign no document unless it states that sit-ins are legal.' In this they were supported by the students' union which at one meeting voted by 376 to 18 to approve a resolution insisting that 'sit-ins and other types of non-violent direct action are legal forms of protest'. A spokesman for the Association for University Participation which consisted of students involved in the sit-in said, 'If the vice-chancellor refuses to back down, the association will call another union meeting and demand a sit-in.' No such sit-in was held.

At some institutions attempts to agitate opinion continued. At Edinburgh copies of a report on the use of the university appointments office of private information available to it on students were stolen, duplicated and circulated. This had happened when 50 students had arrived at the administration offices and demanded to read the report. They had been allowed in four at a time to read it. This investigation stated that although there was an excessive preoccupation with students' social backgrounds $98\frac{1}{2}$ per cent of the appointment board's assessments could not be faulted. At Lancaster, too, purloined documents were an occasion for small-scale discussion. A memorandum alleged to show that Lord Derby, the pro-chancellor, wished to head a special council with powers to send down students appearing in court was circulated in the student magazine, *Spark*. It was also alleged that Lord Derby had differences of opinion with the vice-chancellor, Sir Charles Carter. However no general excitement was created.

The mopping-up was helped by the ebb of the tide at its source. On April 14 Lord Radcliffe, chancellor of Warwick University, stated in his report that no political files had been kept on students or staff. No disciplinary action, however, was to be taken against students involved in the occupation or the thefts. This decision was taken by the senate. A meeting of the students' union immediately refused to accept the Radcliffe Report and said that the university council, the governing body, by accepting it, had 'demonstrated it was totally unfit as a governing body'. It therefore decided to cease communication and correspondence with all officers and committees of the university.

Other reports were produced besides those at Edinburgh and Warwick. The Southampton one blamed the students' union for allowing a minority to make decisions which 'did not reflect majority opinion'. It also stated that 'nothing was achieved that could not have been accomplished by peaceful means'.

Minor disturbances over tangible issues did not disappear entirely. At Bolton Institute of Technology there was a small demonstration when Princess Margaret came to open the building. There were banners and leaflets. One student said that there were 'inadequate facilities and conditions' at Bolton College of Art and Design. At the Camden Institute of Technology, London, a teacher claimed that he had been dismissed for supporting a students' protest against the pottery department's profit-making at students' expense in clay. He claimed that two other teachers had resigned in sympathy, that 150 adult students had signed a petition on his behalf and that he had received a letter of support from the president of L.S.E. students' union.

The N.U.S. had almost sunk from sight during most of the events of April. At its conference early in the month it condemned student use of violence in the Files Controversy. In view of the Great Red Plot theory it must be stated that one of the foremost proponents of the non-violent policy was a communist member of the N.U.S. executive. The non-violent policy was attacked by the delegate from Sussex on the grounds that it implicitly condemned the actions of Warwick, Sussex and Oxford students. A motion was passed enjoining students to 'have the greatest possible disruptive effect on the game' of any South African team playing near them.

No individual university or college union or any individual student allowed its, his or her behaviour to be governed by an N.U.S. decision. However, this disapproval of violence awoke the

hostility of the Extreme Left and when the N.U.S. later refused
to take any positive or direct action to oppose or avenge the disciplining of Oxford, Liverpool, Essex and London students, the
Left headed by the Oxford Campaign for a Democratic University
demonstrated on April 22 outside the N.U.S. offices in London in
the hope of occupying them. The N.U.S. offices were barricaded
and three coachloads of police waited nearby in case of trouble.
There were about 150 demonstrators. This was not a large proportion of the thousands at a dozen institutions who had voted for
solidarity. Thus the frailty of the N.U.S. and the numerical
instability of the Extreme Left was demonstrated.

There were some minor episodes of interest in April. It was
announced that grants to universities were to rise by £13 million
and that dons were to have a 9 per cent pay rise. However the
financial squeeze had hit hard and Bradford was now the only
university to refuse to raise its fees for overseas students. This cost
it £25,000 a year.

The government refused on April 9 to consider the suggestion of
Sir Gerald Nabarro that universities should have special police
forces. Mr. Gerry Fowler, Minister of State at the Education and
Science Department, retorted, 'There is a great deal of hysterical
nonsense from the opposition about this.' During this discussion
Mr. Heffer said, of the Liverpool sit-in, 'In the main the students
acted responsibly. Is it not an absolute scandal that the Liverpool
City Council, Conservative-controlled, should suggest that the
grants should be removed from students who become involved in
sit-ins or actions of this kind?' Mr. Doughty, Conservative M.P.
for Surrey East, took a different view: 'The people of this country
are fed up with seeing rates and taxes they pay being misused by
students.'

The dying-down of the Files Controversy gave extra impetus to
the Stop-the-Seventy-Tour campaign. The Young Liberals
adopted at their conference a motion for 'militant non-violent
direct action'. Preparations were made by the S.T.S.T. to picket
the cricket county championship matches at the beginning of May.
The purpose was to 'educate' the cricket public. The prospect of a
more violent struggle than the Springboks one made the Bishop of
Woolwich cut his links with the Anti-Apartheid Group and the
S.T.S.T. and found his own peaceful protest group.

May began with a march and an occupation by L.S.E. Extreme
Left and the Oxford Campaign for a Democratic University. This
combination attracted about 200 people. This May Day march
went to the N.U.S. offices which were closed for the day. It then
returned to L.S.E. and prevented a union meeting from being
held. The president of the union was struck with a banner reading
'Revolution is the festival of the oppressed'.

Action on behalf of disciplined students failed elsewhere also.
The appeal of the expelled Oxford student was rejected. At Keele
excessive noise at an open air party was to be punished. On the
night of the party the registry and a hall of residence were set on
fire. At Liverpool only two students of the ten sentenced had their
sentences reduced on appeal. At once posters appeared reading
'The pigs won't be moved. Appeals unchanged'. There was a
meeting of 400 students. 200 then went to the Senate House to
ask the vice-chancellor, Mr. Trevor Thomas, to address them.
The doors were locked to keep them out but were reopened under
pressure. A window was broken. The students then wandered
round the administrative block and, two hours later, went away.
The vice-chancellor declined to meet their representatives. At
Essex a non-student was ordered by a High Court judgement never
to set foot on the campus again. He had behaved in a 'threatening
and violent manner'. At Lancaster 49 students were fined £2 each
for their part in publishing purloined documents. Their leader
said, 'We all pleaded not guilty . . . it was a kangaroo court.' The
students demanded that their fines should go to the Pilkington
strikers, Amnesty International, the National Council for Civil
Liberties, the Vietnam Medical Aid Fund or the Stop-the-Seventy-
Tour campaign. The university authorities said, 'It is the university senate who decide where student fines should go.' Unpaid
fines could have meant the refusal of degrees. At Cambridge over
a dozen students were sent for trial on charges connected with the
Garden House Hotel riot in February. 300 other students who had
been present at the riot held a march of complicity and invited the
police to arrest them. At Birmingham 75 students were banned by
High Court order from further occupations of the corporation
offices. They had already occupied these offices twice in protest
against the merging of five colleges to form a polytechnic at Perry
Bar. They wanted a site nearer the university so that they could

have close links with it. At the Architectural Association School the non-renewal of the contract of a member of staff who had proposed a motion of no confidence in the principal provoked but slight and inactive opposition from students.

In this climate of failure and indifference even international matters of note excited little interest. At the beginning of May the U.S.A. extended its Asian war to Cambodia. Several American students were killed in the resulting riots. The demonstration of solidarity held in Britain attracted only 300 people.

As before, Warwick provided an indication of the intensity and success of student activism. The students' union demanded the resignation from the university council of Mr. Gilbert Hunt, the chief executive of the Rootes car firm. So did the senate. So, at a meeting of the Warwick university assembly, did the academic and administrative staff. Their complaint was that he had attempted to influence the university's attitude towards its staff for political reasons. Of 250 entitled to attend this meeting 100 did so. By this time attendance at Warwick students' union meetings was declining. It was soon to become impossible to gain the necessary quorum of 150. When the motion for Mr. Hunt's departure came before the university council, the ultimate authority, it was rejected by 21 votes to 2. There are 8 dons on the council. Excitement had sunk to the point where unwelcome demands could be safely ignored.

This wave of apathy encouraged some of the less 'militant' students to form what they called the Third Force, centred on the Midlands. In the sudden vacuum produced by the collapse of the Extreme Left's power within universities the leaders of the Third Force hoped to make their views prevail. At the North-West regional council of students a motion of support for the March 19 Movement at Liverpool University was voted down. However, it was even more difficult to maintain and organize the Third Force than the Extreme Left. It lacked the glamour of direct action. It faded.

Domestic student disturbances were obscured by national events. The announcement of the General Election and the imminence of the South African cricket tour once more embroiled students in extra-university politics. The threats of the S.T.S.T. became such that elaborate precautions were taken to protect the cricket grounds and the polarization of public opinion already marked during the

Springboks tour became more acute. It is hardly too much to say
that it split the country, or at least the politically conscious section
of its populace. It divided the Labour and Conservative parties
with a sharpness unknown on most issues. The date of arrival of
the South African team was June 18—the day of the General
Election. The pressure on the government to obtain from the
M.C.C. the cancellation of the tour increased. There were more
token disruptions of tennis matches. The Labour Party was
divided on the extent of its dislike of the prospect of the tour.
Some M.P.s were prepared to join in the disruptive activities
planned, but the government felt it to be its duty to insist on the
right of people to play and watch cricket as they wished. By
May 22, however, the government's fear of violence was such that
it asked the M.C.C. to call the tour off. The M.C.C. complied. The
cancellation of the tour aroused deep bitterness among many
people.

The forces planned for the disruption of the South African
matches were primarily student groups, because students, particularly since the tour was to fall in the vacation, would have had the
time and energy to make up a large proportion of the disrupters.
The Springboks episode had demonstrated this clearly. Then
attempts to interest workers, housewives etc. had not met with
success. Student power had affected a decision of government. It
was not individual marches or protests that alarmed the government. In itself the tour's condemnation by the Oxford Union and
the Ruskin College, Oxford, march did not matter. It was the
prospect of a mass consolidation of such groups welded and
inflamed by mob hysteria that caused the government to request
the cancellation of the tour. In this attitude the government was
supported by the Liberals. Immediately after the cancellation of
the tour the Young Liberal leader of the S.T.S.T. announced that
it was not going to disband but to turn its attention to the destruction of commercial links with South Africa.

Meanwhile scholastic communities were considering financial
matters. The vice-chancellors finally rejected all but one of the
economy proposals put forward by the government during the
winter. The Association of University Teachers demanded a pay-
rise of 10 or 15 per cent. The Association of Teachers in Technical
Institutions also made financial claims and demanded a closed

shop. Bullock expressed anxiety about the effect of financial stringency on academic standards. Thus money asserted its importance again.

June began with a meeting of the Students for a Labour Victory. It was intended that thousands of students should flood the marginals. The meeting of June 1 in the University of London Union attracted about 20 people.

The Oxford Union Society announced that it would definitely 'go public' and have the compulsory membership of all registered Oxford University students at £1 a head. Oxford, indeed, had various financial worries. The problem of raising the fees of overseas students continued to divide Congregation. It was not cheered to find that most sixth-formers wanted to go to red-bricks.

The N.U.S. used the lull in Extreme Left-wing agitation within educational institutions to urge students' unions at art colleges and technical institutions to press for representation on governing boards. Since many student bodies had never troubled to organize themselves into unions this was an uphill task. The Department of Education and Science had recently requested college governing bodies to cut their proportion of local authority representation from a third to a quarter and to give the vacant places to staff, students, local trade unionists and employers. This presented obvious difficulties.

The repercussions of previous incidents continued to agitate a few institutions. At Essex 5 students resigned their places on the university senate. Students had 11 of the 40 seats on the senate. The 5 students complained, 'Every decision which has been successfully influenced by students on senates has subsequently been referred back and reversed.' At Keele several students were fined or suspended for playing a record-player at full blast at a midnight party. One had been involved in the files break-in previously. The students' union which had, two weeks earlier, refused to recognize any disciplinary tribunal which did not have 50 per cent student representation took legal action in an attempt to have these sentences revoked. The president of the union said, 'We regard these punishments as being very harsh indeed for what amounts to making a bit of noise.' The registrar said, 'It is clear that the committee and vice-chancellor have taken the view that excessive noise, which deliberately interferes with the right of students at a university to work in peace, is a most serious offence.' Keele had its own customs of disruption. Bands of the Extreme Left would go round aggressively looking as if they were going to cause damage and thus keeping the porters agitated. This was called 'freaking-out'. Many students who did not cause damage or 'freak-out' appeared at union meetings to vote against the condemnation of such activities. The most publicized event of the summer term was nude sun-bathing by some students. This attracted much public attention and condemnation. Eventually the sun-bathers had to pay small fines.

Meanwhile the ghost of a long-dead controversy materialized. At Birmingham an applicant for the post of lecturer in sociology was recommended by the sociology department to the appointments board. This rejected him. The rejection was supported by the unanimous vote of the senate. The applicant had during the 1968 sit-in spoken in encouragement of the occupation and in condonation of the files break-in during the occupation. He had professed himself willing to resign the temporary post which he then held if students were disciplined for their activities in the sit-in. He himself had subsequently taught at Manchester and was now seeking to return to Birmingham. When he was rejected by the university his supporters claimed that he was a brilliant scholar and suited to the demands of the course. It then transpired that his professor at the London School of Economics had refused to accept his thesis. It was alleged that the dispute split the university from top to bottom. Since of the 6,000 students of the institution only 232 went to a union meeting on June 19 when the dispute had been going on for two weeks and since outside the sociology department the staff overwhelmingly did not want the applicant appointed, the allegation may seem a little exaggerated.

The most important event in the month in university as in national life was the Conservative victory in the General Election. It was expected that this would lead to a change in the emphasis of expenditure from higher and further education to primary and secondary schooling.

July was notable for one particular incident. At the beginning of the month half a dozen Cambridge students were gaoled, one for eighteen months, for their part in the Garden House Hotel riot. The leader of Cambridge Council said that feeling in the city was that the sentences were about right. The two Conservative M.P.s for the city felt that the sentences were rather severe. The following month the cases went to the Court of Appeal. The sentences were upheld although one student was sent to a psychiatric hospital instead of to gaol. However two students who had been recommended for deportation were allowed to remain in this country. About two dozen students demonstrated outside the Court with placards enjoining the workers to show solidarity with the students. An attempt to hold a 24-hour vigil in London failed because of lack of support. In Cambridge itself those trying to hold such a vigil were pelted with missiles by skinheads. The judge at the Court of Appeal had said, 'It cannot be too plainly stated or too widely known that the moment a man joins in an attempt to overpower the police who are performing their protective duties that line has been overstepped. . . . Those who act thus against the police . . . must expect custodial sentences.' He was more restrained than Lord Justice Melford Stevenson, who had originally sentenced the students. Lord Justice Melford Stevenson had commented adversely on the encouragement given by some of Cambridge staff to such disruptions. There was a wave of protest at this.

Thus the academic year 1969–70 closed. Like the previous ones it had several climaxes of disturbance and had ended in apathy. The fluctuations in numbers of students taking an active interest in disturbance had been as striking as those of the previous year. The unrest at Warwick had ended in nothing more eventful than the lying-down, at the summer degree ceremony, of various students with ropes round their necks to simulate the strangulation of education. However the limits of tolerance were being widened. The Extreme Left was claiming not only the right to do as it liked in universities but to prevent other people in universities from doing what they wanted even when such activities were legal and non-disruptive. The confidentiality of records had been breached with remarkably little outcry. The Extreme Left had extended its claims to the outside world and assumed the right to tell other people how not to entertain themselves and which sporting teams not to play or to watch. It had claimed the right to resort to unpunished violence when its wishes in this respect were ignored. The year had also seen the failure of the N.U.S. to establish itself as the focus of student loyalty and the organ of student expression.

In view of the heterogeneous nature of the 400,000 students of the country this failure is not surprising.

The autumn of the following academic year showed the continuation of all the trends described. At Cambridge a 'Cambridge students' union' formed itself to abolish the powers of the proctors. The proctors had given evidence in the Cambridge trials. The first meeting attracted over 1,000 students of the 10,000 of Cambridge. Within a month this figure had sunk to half and a projected sit-in was abandoned because of the probable lack of support. The relative moderates at this meeting of 600 were much criticized by their more active colleagues who brought in a large paper dragon. They could not agree on what it represented.

At Keele there was another break-in in the registry and a sit-in of 300 students. These acts were in protest against discipline for offences committed the previous year. There was also a threatening demonstration outside the vice-chancellor's house.

At Birmingham before term began the Left planned to agitate for an occupation on behalf of the lecturer whose application had been rejected. The general indifference—for although 500 people came to a meeting it was not practicable to occupy a large university like Birmingham with less than 1,000—compelled the Extreme Left to change its plan. It hired the lecturer at union expense and tried to have him accepted as a *de facto* member of staff. These attempts were ignored by the authorities.

At Manchester also a lecturer, this time in philosophy, suffered professionally for a speech in favour of the sit-in, at that institution. However, a students' union meeting decided against an occupation as it would be futile. The proportion of potential occupiers was even smaller than at Birmingham. A Council for Academic Freedom and Democracy was set up to contest the decisions of Birmingham and Manchester universities. It was headed by the Professor of English Law at the L.S.E. Its verdicts were predictable and ignored.

At London University an Anti-Imperialist Week was held from October 26 to October 31. It attracted few of London University's 33,000 internal students. A demonstration held to commemorate the anniversary of the previous year's October 27 demonstration had attracted about 400 people. At L.S.E., the original focus of disturbance, the Socialist Society turned to organizing the Gay Liberation Front for homosexuals. It was obvious that the old stimuli had failed to excite further. Student activists were now waiting for a new cause to succeed the dying ones. They found one in December 1970 in the attempt to close Houghton Street to traffic.

Financial difficulties for universities continued. The new Minister for Education and Science planned to extend admission to the Open University, a part-time one relying on correspondence courses and television, to 18-year-olds, thus relieving pressure on the universities. This brought renewed difficulties with the Local Education Authorities who were unwilling to pay grants for these courses. The Chancellor of the Exchequer, Mr. Anthony Barber, was reported to be considering the suggestion that emigrating graduates should pay the cost of their degree courses. This was opposed by the N.U.S. Lord Todd, when addressing the British Association of Scientists, questioned whether it was desirable to extend university education to so many. He said that some were not capable of benefiting from it and that such education was really suited to the creative élite. There was an immediate outcry from the 'progressive' section of the academic world. When the Third Black Paper was published a couple of months later there was another outcry. In other words the controversy continued. So did the student swing away from the physical sciences. All the tensions in universities continued unrelieved.

The belief of the student Extreme Left that it had a right to intervene in the activities of other students was strengthened. In October 1970 York University students' union voted £720 to various Left-wing organizations, £80 to the Conservative Association and nothing to the Monday Club. The president of the union said that the students had decided that they 'did not support the views of the Monday Club and did not wish those views propagated within this university'. At Goldsmith's College, London, the Conservative Association invited Mrs. Thatcher to come and address a closed meeting of the Association. She accepted. The students' union then declared that in view of the importance of the speaker's theme—'Education'—and position the meeting should be open. In view of the glasses hurled at a previous Conservative meeting addressed by a controversial speaker the Conservatives were not enthusiastic.

The Barclays Bank Controversy continued. The University of

East Anglia students' union decided to cut all links with the authorities until all the university's accounts were removed from this bank.

1970–1971 showed every sign of repeating the pattern of its predecessors.

5

The Mechanics of Disruption

THE PRECEDING chapters have described the sequence of student disturbances of the two years 1968–1970. No complete account can be given in a short book but it is hoped that enough facts have been provided to answer the question, 'What exactly is going on in our universities?' The variety of occasions of disruption and the width of geographical distribution makes generalization difficult but it can safely be said that nearly all the disturbances were the work of minorities. The figures make this clear. When it is pointed out by student opponents of disruption that only a minority of students is actively disruptive people naturally enquire how this minority imposes its will on the student body as a whole.

The immediate answers to this question are easily listed. If the Extreme Left can, it gives its policies of disruption the sanction of approval by the students' union. Since most students do not want disturbance this might seem difficult. However a long meeting wears down the opponents of disruption. At Liverpool in 1970 the proposal to occupy the administration block was debated for five hours. At L.S.E. also meetings sometimes lasted as long. One indeed lasted five and a half hours. The largest L.S.E. union meeting ever held attracted over 1,700 people; after five hours they voted for the establishment of a committee of 23 all except one of whom were members of the Socialist Society and against going on a march immediately after the meeting. They were very hungry and wanted to finish the deliberations as quickly as possible.

A similar tactic has been frequency of meetings. Union meetings were held one after another until the proposal for direct action was adopted. In the week ending in the destruction of the gates at L.S.E. there were four union meetings. After the reopening of the

L.S.E. in February 1969 a proposal for occupation was brought up at three successive meetings before being adopted. The vote for occupation remained roughly constant—about 360—but the vote against occupation fell from 686 to 415 to 206. At Southampton the Extreme Left tried by forcing a whole series of meetings to bring successfully a motion excluding Major Patrick Wall.

Tactics of this nature were summarized in a letter published in *The Times* on January 28, 1969. An L.S.E. post-graduate wrote of the Extreme Left, 'They are attempting to impose change on the nature of the community by the technique of calling continual meetings until, by the weariness of the other students, they are able to get a majority at one particular meeting. This tactic pays even more dividends when the Press and the B.B.C. misinterpret the result.' Similar letters appeared in the local Press. During the Birmingham occupation of November–December 1968 a student wrote in the *Birmingham Post* the following letter:

Because of the present state of affairs at Birmingham University I (as a student there) feel compelled to hit back at the publicity which the militants are receiving.

These people are skilled politicians in the sense that they know all the tricks by which they can appear to have a majority of the students behind them.

For instance they call meetings at times when only people who are prepared to miss lectures or a meal can attend. If this fails they wait until those opposed to them are not present in sufficient numbers to outvote them. They hide behind the constitutional technicalities of the Guild.

The rest of us find ourselves forced to go to meetings which take place almost daily to vote against the militants who would otherwise have a constitutional majority which is then said to represent us all.

This is more or less what happened on November 28th at the meeting which voted for direct action. Most of us did not realise what this meeting was about nor that its consequences would be what they are.

Now that we realise how we have been tricked—quite constitutionally—we are desperately trying to reverse the decisions already taken by constitutional means.

There is a hard core of about 50 militants who have managed to lead some of our more feeble-minded colleagues astray.

Another tactic practised in some places was by vigorous persuasion applied to the president of the union and his executive to convert without notice a 'general assembly' called by the Left into a union meeting with powers to commit the student body. This was how one of the union meetings immediately preceding the destruction of L.S.E. gates was formed. Another tactic was to propose without notice a disruptive policy of which the student body would certainly disapprove. This was how L.S.E. Left succeeded in March 1969 in having a proposal for occupation adopted by the union. Yet another tactic, criticized in the letter just quoted, was to have union meetings held at times inconvenient for most students. This particularly affected science students who keep to a rigid time-table—and who tend to vote, if at all, against disruption.

A factor favouring manipulation of students' unions was the low-ness of the quorum at most universities, At Birmingham and York it was 75, at Manchester and University College, London, 100, and at Warwick and L.S.E., 150. In many cases the quorum had to be low in order to hold students' union meetings at all. The fear of indifference was a greater force than the fear of disturbance. It is significant that after a period of disruption the quorum was raised in some cases. In March 1970 the quorum at Manchester was raised from 100 to 200. Several months earlier the L.S.E. quorum had been raised from 60 to 150.

The Report of the Commons select committee on the problems of higher education stated that the constitutions of students' unions allowed them to be used in this fashion. The Report deplored this custom and suggested that it should be changed. A report on the difficulties of Southampton University in particular made the same point.

There were many tactics connected with these types of mani-pulation of union meetings. Outsiders were introduced to vote for and carry out acts of disruption. Three of the 13 people charged with destroying L.S.E. gates were not L.S.E. students. The two men who seized the microphone at L.S.E. Oration Day in 1969 were not students. The vice-chancellor of Manchester University alleged that some of the instigators of trouble at his institution were not Manchester University students. In a meeting it was impossible to tell, when it came to counting votes, who were students and who were not.

There was also the tactic of forcing elections to union offices. Frequent elections like frequent meetings wore down the opponents of disruption. By making life intolerable for union representative councils the Extreme Left could force them to resign. At the L.S.E. in November 1969 Mr. Colin Crouch, the president, was forced to resign in this manner. The council also resigned. In the consequent election there was a poll of 1,400. All the posts were won by the opponents of disruption. However the next term when the process was repeated the poll was about 1,300 for the presidency but much less for the other posts—except for two which were not contested at all. Except for the presidency most of the posts went to the Extreme Left. To the public it looked like a swing to the Extreme Left. In fact it was a concealed swing to apathy. This was made even clearer in the elections to the student places on the general purposes committee. The victors in these elections were leaders of the Extreme Left and received about 400 votes each.

Similar harassment of presidents and executive councils took place at Bristol where in 1969 the president resigned saying that the Extreme Left had thrown the whole student body into confusion and at Exeter where in 1970, as previously stated, the president said that the Extreme Left had 'consistently pointed a pistol' at him and the executive.

There were places in which geography helped the Extreme Left. At L.S.E. any meeting of over 700 had to be held in several rooms connected by tannoy. The focus and biggest room was the Old Theatre. The Extreme Left would arrive first and fill most of it. This was useful when votes of acclamation were taken. It was obviously impossible to add up several sets of acclamation so voting in this fashion took place in the Old Theatre only. This was how in October 1968 a proposal for declaring the union neutral towards an occupation was adopted although the meeting was against it.

Thus union meetings were manipulated. There were, however, standbys for when union meetings could not be manipulated directly. Direct action could be taken in the expectation that an appeal to student solidarity would secure its later ratification at a union meeting. This was how the Birmingham and Warwick sit-ins began. Entirely new organizations could be set up claiming to be unions and representing the students of the institution. This was what happened at the Inns of Court in November 1968 and at Cambridge in October 1970. Neither group represented more than a fraction of the students of their institutions or had any official and corporate existence.

If none of these tactics worked the Extreme Left defied the unions. The Liverpool sit-in was started in defiance of a union vote. The Bristol sit-in was continued despite a union vote of 773 to 215 with 87 abstentions. At L.S.E. the visit of the Commons select committee was disrupted in defiance of the vote just taken at a union meeting. At Leeds Major Wall's speech was disturbed in spite of the union's vote in favour of free speech. When student unions could not be manipulated they were described as un-representative bureaucracies and were ignored or attacked by the Extreme Left. This was clear at L.S.E. in March 1969 when a proposal for occupation was being debated. In answer to a question the proposer of the motion said that even if the occupation was voted down officially it would take place. The following year attempts at occupation were made without union sanction. This was partly because the quorum for union meetings could not be maintained. Wearing people down had its disadvantages.

A tactic combining both the constitutional and the unconstitu-tional was to compound the two and give legality to the whole. Birmingham provided the most interesting example of this. The sit-in had been started unofficially by the *ad hoc* committee of the Extreme Left. It had then been adopted by the guild executive council. A guild meeting, however, elected a committee of ten to run the sit-in which had a brief autonomous life. Thus there was a variety of authorities and the coincidence of policy among them seemed to legitimize the unofficial authorities. There was also an action committee of opponents of disruption.

This confusion was reflected in meetings. It was difficult for students to know which meeting had the most authority. On December 2 an unofficial midday meeting of two thousand oppo-nents of the sit-in condemned it. On the evening of the same day an unofficial meeting of the same size of the occupiers decided to continue the sit-in. On December 3 an official 4,000-strong meeting of the students' Guild voted to end the sit-in. That night, after a five-and-a-half-hour meeting, the guild executive council which claimed to be the policy-making body voted by 71 to 42 to continue the sit-in. The following day an official guild meeting decided to oppose discipline. Since this meeting numbered only 2,000 and an unofficial one held the same day had attracted 1,000 and since only 70 or 80 were now occupying the buildings overnight in contrast to the 500 or so who had slept there at the beginning of the sit-in the occupation was called off with the aid of a face-saving compromise. The whole Birmingham sit-in illustrates the protean quality of disruption and the brevity of its life.

There is nothing to prevent disruption once started from running its full course. The examples above indicate the more obvious reasons. Those students hostile to disruption can neither prevent nor curtail it. The university authorities have no physical force at their disposal. Legal proceedings against disrupters are slow and cumbersome. The police are usually unwilling to intervene, as the cases of L.S.E. and Bristol show. Thus disruption can continue until its supporters tire of it. This is why summer terms contain few disturbances and more punishments for previous disturbances. This is in its turn why disruption becomes more extreme. When a march would look unimpressive because of the slightness of support then an occupation—which, taking place in a small area, looks better-supported—must be tried. When an occupation would be insufficiently supported then actual destruction must be committed to make an impact. One of the mistakes made by L.S.E. Left in 1969 was to succeed an ineffective occupation with an ineffective strike, for a strike needs far more support than an occupation to make itself felt. Thus the forms of disruption change with the amount of support available or expected.

It must be mentioned also that tactics included violence and the threat of violence, libellous leaflets, suppression of the leaflets of opponents and other discouragements of resistance. At L.S.E. and the City University libel action was considered against the authors, if found, of such publications. At L.S.E. an attempt was made to seize a petition of opponents of disruption, the correspondence of a leading opponent was intercepted and Right-wing candidates for office were prevented from using the students' union duplicating machine for their leaflets. At Birmingham leaflets being distributed by the opponents of disruption were seized by the Extreme Left. At L.S.E. a van-driver who brought food into the college in defiance of the boycott was assaulted. When L.S.E. Extreme Left occupied the University of London Union its supporters seized by force from the L.U. officials the keys to the buildings.

Thus by unceasing pressure and manoeuvre the Extreme Left over the two years 1968–70 forced its policies on student bodies although it constituted only a small minority in every one of the institutions in which it was active.

6

The 'Moderates'

THE PREVIOUS chapter listed some of the techniques of manipulation. However these techniques do not by themselves explain the inability of those opposed to disruption to make their view prevail. The real answer to the question 'Why don't the moderates do something?' lies deeper.

The first thing that must be said is that there were no moderates in the sense meant by the Press. There were two groups of students opposed to disruption—the muddle-headed and the constitutionalists. The constitutionalists believed that the disrupters should be expelled. The muddle-headed believed that they should stop disrupting but should not be punished for any act of disruption. It is this group to whom the label 'moderate' is best applied for it constituted the majority of students who went to any meetings at all though not of those who went to regular meetings. The biggest of all student political groups was that of the totally apathetic.

The 'moderates' were a heterogeneous group. There was a wide variety of attitudes towards disruption and any communal letter or petition from them was carefully phrased. A collective letter to *The Times* from opponents of the Birmingham sit-in stated, 'The motive for our action in initiating this letter is to show that by no means all students at this university agree with the methods adopted by student militants, though some of its signatories were broadly in sympathy with their aims.' A proposal put forward by Bristol 'moderates' at a students' union meeting was similarly cautious, 'We, the undersigned, while we may sympathize with the idea of reciprocal membership, object to the present occupation of the Senate House.' The 'moderates' sometimes seemed to condemn disruption but not the disrupters. In a political sense they tended to be on the Left wings of the Labour and Liberal parties or to the Left of those. This should indicate some of the peculiarities of the university political spectrum.

Although the 'moderates' constituted an absolute majority over the Extreme Left and the constitutionalists together they were unable to use this power. Their interest in student politics was too spasmodic for them to develop cohesion, organization or clarity of purpose. They were always the first to retreat to the libraries.

All the techniques of disruption would have been useless if the 'moderates' had been determined and clear-headed. They could have changed the constitutions of their unions and thus made manipulation more difficult. They could have refused to support sit-ins. They could have supported the authorities' attempts at discipline. The best illustration of this is from the L.S.E. occupation of October 1968. The 'moderates' were less concerned to prevent the occupation than the Extreme Left were to hold it. So the Extreme Left arrived first and arranged themselves to the best advantage. When the occupation began—on a minority vote of the students' union—and the director of the L.S.E. declared the School closed many of those who had just voted against the occupation and seen their votes ignored by the Extreme Left now joined the occupation. It is some indication of the lack of energy of the 'moderates' that although there were 1,000 signatures on the petition organized to call a union meeting to oppose the occupation only two-thirds of these attended the meeting when it was held. This pattern of resistance followed by support was repeated the following term when the gates were destroyed after a small meeting and a narrow majority. The Friends' House meeting of February 3, 1969 held during the L.S.E. closure decided that it regretted that such destruction had been necessary. The same meeting, consisting largely of 'moderates', promised solidarity with students threatened with discipline although it knew of the thefts and acts of violence just committed by the Extreme Left during the occupation of U.L.U. It knew also that once back in L.S.E. the Extreme Left would continue trying to push policies of violence through union meetings and would ignore union votes against such policies. It knew also that most 'moderates' would not turn out to vote against such policies.

Similar attitudes were displayed by 'moderates' in other institutions. Essex students' union condemned legal action taken against 40 students for obstruction in Colchester. At Liverpool the students' union first opposed and then criticized the sit-in; but when students were disciplined the 'moderates' changed their attitude, and made the same demands as the Extreme Left had. At Birmingham the breaking-open of the files was overlooked by the 'moderates' in their support of the occupation begun without their being consulted. At Warwick the following year there was also little disapproval of similar thefts. The same effective condonation was given by Edinburgh students' representative council.

Similar self-deception was employed in the controversy over the expression of opinions unpopular in university circles. When Major Wall was shouted down at York University in November 1968, attempts were made by the president of the union to smooth matters over. 'We hope to reach agreement among all sections of the university community about the way in which university meetings should be conducted.' The president said the Extreme Left had thought there was to be no discussion after Major Wall's speech and this belief had helped to cause the trouble. It is difficult to believe that he seriously thought that if promised a discussion afterwards the Extreme Left would have listened quietly to Major Wall's speech. The president hoped for agreement between opposing political societies not to disrupt each other's meetings. It salves the 'Left-wing' consciences of some students if Right-wingers could also be criticized, if not for disruption at least for the possibility, however slight, that they might commit disruption. The president of Southampton University union was more indulgent to those of his colleagues who shouted Lord Beeching down. 'When you have only once chance you do tend to press your point.' The same ambivalence was apparent in the attitude of the N.U.S. executive which maintained virtual silence on the propriety or otherwise of such disruptions of political meetings. The Extreme Left claimed that to support the right of Mr. Powell, Major Wall, Lord Beeching or Mr. Michael Stewart to speak was to support their views, and this claim made many 'moderates' irresolute.

No students' union meeting at any institution has ever actually advocated discipline. The nearest approach to this was at L.S.E.

in May 1969 when the disruption of lectures was condemned—
with no suggestion of how to prevent its repetition.

Thus the Extreme Left could hope for the tacit support of the
'moderates'. However they never managed to make this support
effective. At L.S.E. the spokesman of the Extreme Left enquired,
'Where are those who voted with us at the Friends' House?' The
answer was simple. They were in the Library. At Liverpool the
'moderates' confined their protest against the sentences inflicted
on the Extreme Left to a one-day boycott. At Nottingham meetings
became too small to start mass occupations. At Birmingham the
promise by a 2,000-strong meeting to oppose discipline had long
been forgotten by the time it was appealed to. At Hull the president
of the union elected on the 'Vote academic thug!' slogan was forced
to resign as he could not carry the union with him. The fact was
that promises of 'moderate' support made at moments of excitement were quickly forgotten.

The 'moderates' did not really like to admit that they were
opposed to disruption. This would have been 'Right-wing' and as
such to be avoided like the plague. The 'moderates' were the
victims of self-deception, inconsistency and confusion. They
seemed to believe in the mystic brotherhood of all those with the
qualifications for higher or further education. However they did
not intend to act positively on this belief.

The 'moderates' tended to salve their consciences of the stain of
opposing disruption by asserting their student status in demands
for student representation. However they did not really want
much student participation, let alone power or responsibility.
L.S.E. provided the most striking example of this. The Friends'
House meeting of about 1,700 students voted unanimously for
more student representation yet in the union elections less than a
month later fewer than 1,000 bothered to vote (though over 1,300
voted for the president's post). They did not want to exercise power
through meetings which they did not like; and they would not vote
for representatives let alone stand for office. Recruitment for staff-
student committees was usually a difficult task. It was even more
difficult to find students to sit on finance and constitution committees. The 'moderates' did not think through the implications
of the policies for which they voted. The result was that in many
elections to newly created student representative posts the Extreme

5

Left were opposed energetically only by the constitutionalists who did know what they wanted. The swifter the multiplication of student representative posts the greater was the swing to apathy and the easier the acquisition of these posts by the Extreme Left, who could, however, make no use of them because of this same apathy. When election polls at L.S.E. had sunk to 200 it did not matter who won since those elected would represent no one except themselves and would be unable to appeal to mass support. The 'moderates' would not admit that they did not really want participation.

These tendencies were general as the other institutions subject to disruption showed. Soon after the Birmingham occupation one meeting was inquorate. The following year the poll for the presidency fell by half to 1,101 of the 6,000 students. This was hardly an indication of widespread student aspirations to share in the running of the university. At Manchester the union meeting immediately before the outbreak of the Files Controversy was inquorate. The quorum was then 100. By June 1970, after the sit-in, the annual general meeting attracted a bare quorum. The quorum was then 200. The presidential poll was usually less than 3,000. There are 11,000 students at the university. At University College, London, after the march in October 1969 on behalf of the American revolutionary student at Bedford interest in student politics sank so low that the union council was worried and tried to introduce changes to remedy this.

These tendencies did not pass unnoticed at the time. At the Regent Street Polytechnic, London, Sir Eric Richardson, director of the board of governors, said that students did not show much interest in committees. Sir Hugh Robson, vice-chancellor of Sheffield University, doubted whether a tenth of his student body took any serious or consistent interest in university matters. However most people did not dwell on these low attendances and polls. Within universities it would have been considered 'Right-wing' to oppose the increase in student representative posts merely because it was difficult to fill those already instituted.

Thus it would be unreasonable to claim that the desire for student representation by the 'moderates' was the lever used by the Extreme Left to shake educational institutions. The 'moderates' discovered these aspirations when they wished to prove that they were 'Left-wing' even if they did not want to riot. Demands for representation were usually made not by the 'moderates', very few of whom were capable of making a speech or writing a clear account of what they wanted, but by the constitutionalists who used this 'moderate' self-deception in order to stave off immediate disruption.

The Extreme Left alleged that low polls and attendances were due to lack of student power and claimed that the exercise of real power would attract students. They said that the posts offered were useless and realized to be so. If this had been the case and there had indeed been a strong movement for participation amounting to power the 'moderates' would have pressed persistently for it. When 5 Essex student representatives resigned from the senate on the grounds that they were always outvoted and that their posts were therefore useless there was no mass move to press for more genuinely powerful positions.

It must also be stressed that the amount of student representation did not blunt the edge of disruption. Once obtained particular representative posts went unappreciated and indeed unnoticed. Sussex, Bradford, Keele, Essex and Nottingham had all granted a substantial measure of student representation before their most violent troubles broke out. Manchester was in the process of working out how student influence could be integrated into the administration when its sit-ins began. Lancaster, like Sussex and Bradford, had students on the senate.

The further up the academic hierarchy, the greater was the indifference to student politics. Ph.D. students were too busy to join in. This was particularly true at the L.S.E. where the Graduate Students' Association had 1,000 members in name. Apart from some M.Sc. and M.A. students most never came to meetings. In the year 1968 the G.S.A.'s executive posts were filled on a poll of 8 per cent. In 1969 the elections were not contested. The posts were therefore filled by the Extreme Left. They found it difficult to reach the quorum of 30 for association meetings. On one occasion an appeal had to be made in the nearest canteen for enough graduates to make up the quorum. This did not, however, prevent demands for student power. It is fair to say that just as L.S.E. in general saw the greatest disruption it also saw the greatest apathy. The last union meeting of the academic year

1969–70 attracted 17 people. The president waited in the hope that more would come but the number sank to 15 so he closed the meeting. There are sound reasons for the reluctance of university authorities to entrust great power to student meetings or representatives.

It is clear that on a wide range of matters from discipline to representation the 'moderates' did not mean what they said, or allowed to be said in their names. Their demands were as unreal as those of the Extreme Left. They closed their eyes to the violence and dishonesty of the Extreme Left; the tactics of force, manipulation and misrepresentation would have been self-defeating if the 'moderates' had not usually felt guilty at disapproving openly of such action when they were 'Left-wing'. The 'moderates' constantly fell for moral blackmail. When they were told that to condemn disruption or oppose an occupation was 'Right wing', 'anti-student' or 'fascist' they were deceived. The Left-wing tactic of linking two entirely unconnected matters and claiming that support for one policy implied support for the other was only successful because of the confusion and irresolution of the 'moderates'. In this way the Extreme Left at L.S.E. claimed that to oppose occupations was to take the line that Mr. Ian Smith, 'Prime Minister' of the 'Republic of Rhodesia', would have taken.

Thus the 'moderates' were essentially passive, pushed first one way and then the other by more vigorous groups and finally pushed into the Library by the imminence of the summer examinations. They were led and ignored by the Extreme Left and the constitutionalists according to the mood of the moment. They deserved the opinion held of them by both groups.

The 'moderate' vote counted in union polls, but not in union meetings. Thus a president elected by a 'moderate' vote would often face a hostile assembly. Mr. Colin Crouch, when resigning from the presidency of L.S.E. union, said that there just wasn't enough enthusiasm among people to come to meetings. His successor yielded to Extreme Left demands to call an unconstitutional meeting and asserted in answer to a question that the union had the right to discuss any project, legal or illegal. When, however, the gates were destroyed he resigned from the presidency because of the probable legal consequences. Such was the dilemma of 'moderation'. The next president, Mr. Christopher Pryce, had advocated 'the course of natural justice' for disrupters. The Friends' House meeting overwhelmingly opposed it. He abandoned it, stood for the vacant presidency and won. He took no action when students were disciplined. His election salved the 'Left-wing' consciences of the 'moderates' without committing the union to effective action.

Thus it can be seen that the 'moderates' did not stop disruption because they lacked the moral courage or consistency to do so. The 'moderates' did nothing effectively. They had no positive policy. In every institution there were 'moderates' but their weaknesses allowed Extreme Left minorities to control them or wear them down. The moral weakness of the 'moderates' helped disruption—and its collapse.

7

The Constitutionalists

DISTINCT FROM the 'moderates', though often lumped together with them in the judgement of the public, were the constitutionalists. These students believed that violence and disruption should be punished by suspension or expulsion. They often voted with, and indeed used, the 'moderates' to resist disruption but unlike the 'moderates' did not sanction disruption once it had taken place. They existed in all institutions but sometimes did not publicly press their views. On December 3, 1968 one Birmingham student wrote in the *Birmingham Evening Mail*, 'It is my view that those taking part in the present disgraceful performance should be instantly sent down and removed from the premises of the university.' The letter was unsigned.

The constitutionalists were influenced by a wide variety of pressures and motives. Some feared that disruption would spoil their chances of obtaining a good degree; some feared that employers might be reluctant to take the products of institutions known to be centres of disturbance. In general, however, hard-line opposition to disruption was based on principle. Although it contained many Labour and Liberal voters and some students who found the Conservative party too socialistic it is fair to say that opposition to disruption tended to centre round Conservative Associations. There was a band of opinion from the Fabian Society to the Monday Club which believed that unpopular speakers had a right to be heard, that all points of view should be given in university courses, that academic decisions should be taken by the staff and that students did not have a special dispensation to break the law. There were in addition groups like the George Currie Society in Cambridge, which also had a University Free Speech

Association, and the Oxford Group for Order and Democracy. Opposition to disruption tended to concentrate round more orthodox groups.

Thus the students known to the public as 'moderates' contained not only the irresolute Left-wing students but hard-line constitutionalists and these constitutionalists in their turn contained Right-wingers both inside and outside the Conservative party. It must be pointed out that the hard-liners were all constitutionalists in the sense that they did not retaliate in kind. Despite the advice of Mr. John Braine, the author, to the Monday Club no Left-wing meeting was disrupted.

Opposition to disruption was usually at its most vigorous and best-organized where disruption was most frequent and violent. The most obvious example is that of L.S.E. in the year 1968–69. However the following year saw far less student hard-line opposition to disruption. Warwick, Liverpool and Manchester had no such large opposition groups when their institutions were shaken by disruption.

Thus the hard-line opposition to disruption was to some extent divided along political lines and Labour and Liberal constitutionalists sometimes felt a deep repugnance to doing anything done by Conservatives also. It made them feel tarred by the Right. Some university Labour clubs like those of Cambridge and Birmingham were swallowed by the Extreme Left. Whatever Liberal students thought as individuals the collective view of the Union of Liberal Students was 'moderate'. These divisions and uncertainties weakened the hard-line opposition to disruption. Inevitably it became identified with the Right. In these tendencies the university political parties mirrored their parent parties outside.

Conservative students were not united or consistent. Indeed the Federation of Conservative Students which had a membership of 13,000 seemed at first as ambivalent and irresolute as the 'moderates'. In December 1968 Mr. Ian Taylor, then chairman of the F.C.S., made the following statement of the Birmingham sit-in: 'The university council by refusing to listen to moderate demands have forced students to take direct action. The sit-in has moderate aims and to continue resisting the students' demands will make it more difficult for responsible student leaders to maintain control, as they are doing at the moment.' This statement was

made after the blockading of the vice-chancellor in his office and
after the breaking-open of the files. In the Birmingham local press
the chairman of Aston University Conservative Association supported the Birmingham sit-in. Birmingham University Conservative Association was divided. This same ambivalence was obvious
at the Conservative Party Conference of 1968 when Mr. Taylor
asked delegates not to 'knock students' too much. Mr. Taylor's
views were not shared by all his members. His statement on the
Birmingham sit-in brought vigorous complaints from the Conservatives of King's College, London. Thus the most likely source
of opposition to disruption was itself divided and unsure at the
beginning of the two years from 1968 to 1970. It is some indication
of the intensity of political interest in universities that with 13,000
members the F.C.S. has been the largest political group among the
400,000 hypothetical members of the N.U.S.

However succeeding months saw the hardening of the F.C.S.
line. By the end of April 1969 Mr. Taylor, who was an L.S.E.
student, was not only advocating the 'course of natural justice' in
his own college but 'firm action' in general at a Conservative
seminar on higher education. Mr. Osband, chairman of L.S.E.
Conservative Association, suggested the institution of formal rules
and powers of discipline. The views expressed at this seminar by
Sir Edward Boyle, usually of middle-of-the-road opinions, have
already been quoted. Growing violence and the refusal of the
Extreme Left to allow some Conservative M.P.s to speak in universities hardened the attitude of Conservative students. In
October 1969 an F.C.S. statement condoned sit-ins provided that
they were not disruptive. This was criticized in some quarters as
muddle-headed but it was in fact a realistic approach, for in order
to maintain the tension holding an occupation together acts of
disruption nearly always were committed during sit-ins. The
F.C.S. maintained unswervingly that whatever divisions it might
have about the merits of Mr. Powell's views Mr. Powell had a
right to propound those views, that Conservative associations had
a right to invite him to universities and that university authorities
had a duty to enforce order on these and other occasions. By 1970
the Conservative associations of universities had become the hard
core of the constitutionalists.

It was otherwise with Labour and Liberal students. Some of the reasons for this have already been mentioned. These divisive weakening tendencies became more apparent with the approach of the General Election of 1970. The 'Students for a Labour Victory' represented not the mainstream of Labour opinion but its far Left. The organizer of the S.L.V. in Paddington South had voted in support of the condonation of the violent disruption of lectures at L.S.E. Some of the Young Liberals were planning the violent disruption of the South African cricket tour. It is difficult to escape the conclusion that anxiety to appeal to the young prevented the Labour and Liberal parties from dispensing with the aid of these allies and so gave them respectability. There seemed, in so far as either Labour or Liberal students had any cohesion in their organizations, to be a turn to the Left.

The constitutionalists were most vigorous at L.S.E. This institution had in the year 1968–69 one of the largest Conservative associations of any London college. Its 160 members provided many of the executive of the F.C.S. Perhaps being a Conservative at L.S.E. was a test of faith and determination. In practice the opposition to disruption and the carrying through the union of proposals accepting co-operation with the authorities was organized by the Conservative Association. In October 1969 L.S.E. authorities offered the students' union six places on the court of governors. The union refused by about 220 votes to 190. The meeting had coincided with the Conservative party conference. Thus the most likely organizers of support for this compromise were away. This was a reversal of the policy of the previous November when another motion accepting seats on committees was passed because of the absence of many of the Socialist Society at an R.S.S.F. conference. On such accidents turned the progress of representation. Neither meeting was substantially attended by the 'moderates' who were alleged to want representation. L.S.E. Conservative Association contained many energetic opponents of disruption. Mr. Francis Dobbyn began speeches with, 'Ladies and Gentlemen . . .' He asserted that the way for students to behave towards the disputed gates was to act like reasonable, sensible adults and not create such disorder that the gates would be used. This injunction occasioned immediate uproar. Mr. Richard Osband, chairman in 1968–69, once introduced a motion for the 'course of natural justice' in the face of such strong disapproval that even the Socialist Society chairman of the meeting was compelled to remonstrate as the missiles intended for Mr. Osband were hitting the Socialist Society chairman as well. Mr. Roger Collier and Mr. Len Harris gave evidence against those charged with disruption. Mr. Stephen Kreppel once told a meeting that the authorities were not entirely wrong all the time. No one could accuse L.S.E. Conservatives of lacking the courage of their convictions. This, indeed, applied to their general political views. In November 1968 Mr. Adrian Day, chairman 1970–71, tried to start an Anglo-Rhodesian club. There was a wide spectrum of opinion in L.S.E. Conservative Association.

Of the other 100 or so hard-line opponents of disruption most were Labour or Liberal supporters, if they had any political interests. One, however, Mr. Stephen Maxwell, was a Scottish Nationalist. One of the Extreme Left was a Welsh Nationalist so nationalism could not be claimed as the possession of the constitutionalists or the Extreme Left alone. In the Liberal Association a published statement by Mr. John Robinson about the October 1968 occupation caused his removal from office. He had objected to the waste of university places by some of the Extreme Left. The Labour Association was a paper organization. At its 1969 election for the chairmanship ten people voted. This was one-tenth of the number voting for the chairman of the Conservative Association. Both the constitutionalist presidents of the union of 1968–69, Mr. Crouch and Mr. Pryce, were members of the Labour Association but were unable or unwilling to influence its policy. Mr. Pryce knew his 'moderate' electorate. When bringing forward proposals for accepting seats on committees he always began his speech with a denunciation of the authorities and worked round to the suggestion that accepting the seats offered would turn out to be a blow against the authorities. Thus the constitutionalists of L.S.E. were a varied group, in motive, fervour and method alike.

Other London Conservative groups expressed themselves frankly on disruption. The Conservatives of University College stated those guilty of violence at L.S.E. should be sent down. The most hard-line were at King's.

York Conservative Association was vigorous in its opposition to student violence. One of its members, Mr. Harvey Proctor, became, on graduating, assistant to the director of the Monday Club. Its views on students and the law were strongly expressed. 'We believe that those who feel it necessary to break the law should have the courage of their convictions and not expect hurriedly-convened student meetings, attended by less than one-sixth of the student body, to pay their fines and legal costs out of ratepayers' money.' On the shouting-down of unpopular speakers the association was equally explicit. 'Universities should not be the incubators of organized student thuggery supported by the undergraduate misfits and the overall lack of control and cowardice shown by some university authorities.' There was also little evidence of fraternal solidarity between the Socialist Society and the Conservative Association during the Files Controversy.

A similar line was taken by Leeds Conservative Association which invited both Mr. Ronald Bell and Major Patrick Wall to address it. 11 per cent of Leeds students thought Mr. Powell the greatest politician in Britain. Manchester and Sheffield Conservatives were more cautious and decided not to invite Mr. Powell to speak on university or union property.

It is an interesting reflection that the opponents of disruption were sometimes fairer and more dispassionate than their counterparts. Oxford Conservatives condemned attacks on the police and disruption within universities. Its most prominent figures, Mr. Timothy Smith and Mr. Stephen Milligan, became well-known. Yet Mr. Milligan stated publicly that many of the leaders of the Extreme Left were extremely intelligent and articulate. When Mr. Milligan was president of the Oxford Union a motion supporting the disruption of the South African cricket tour was debated and lost by a narrow margin. There were allegations that the vote had been 'fiddled'. These allegations were investigated and proved to have been well-founded, those responsible claiming that their behaviour was traditional. Mr. Milligan had the debate held again and the motion, of which he personally could hardly have approved, was carried.

A similar quality was displayed by Mr. Sam Wiggs, a Southampton opponent of disruption, who claimed that the failings of the Extreme Left at his institution did not include intellectual inadequacy. He said that the Extreme Left did well at examinations. When Lord Beeching was shouted down at Southampton some students pointed out that the Socialist Society was over-represented in the audience because most other students were preparing for examinations. The results of the examinations were such that the Socialist Society demanded a re-sit.

Perhaps the most determined opponent of disruption was the Liverpool student who before an almost entirely hostile meeting of well over 1,000 stated that those just disciplined deserved it. As has been mentioned earlier he was shouted down.

The institution which provided the clearest illustration of the difficulties confronting the hard-line opposition to disruption was Sussex. There the Conservative Association, though united in its insistence that Major Patrick Wall had a right to speak on the university premises, was openly divided in its attitude to Conservative policy. During the 1969 Conservative Party Conference, held at Brighton, Mr. John Ormowe, Secretary of Sussex Conservative Association, helped to put a full page advertisement in the local paper in support of Mr. Powell's replacement of Mr. Heath, as leader of the Conservative Party. By four votes to two he was asked by Sussex Conservatives' executive committee to resign his secretaryship. At Sussex University the Right was not only small but fragmented in unpleasing circumstances. The constitutionalism of some of the Right seemed tactical rather than heartfelt.

Thus over the two years 1968–70 hard-core opposition to disruption was not successful. Those who ceased to support or condone disruption did not actually become constitutionalists. The 'moderates' were the first to desert student politics for the libraries. They were followed by the constitutionalists and then by the Extreme Left. The constitutionalists failed to win the 'moderates' for active opposition to disruption. This was partly because of the taint of the Right implied, to the 'moderates', by the constitutionalists' defence of free speech, even when the liberal constitutionalists, both inside and outside the Conservative Party, did not approve of the speaker.

Once their initial hesitations had been overcome the Conservatives opposed disruption, but they were handicapped by the inconsistencies of Labour and Liberal students. By the time of the Files Controversy the constitutionalists had lost confidence. It is, however, fair to say that whatever courage, clear-sightedness and consistency were shown by British students in those two years were to be found in the constitutionalists rather than in the 'moderates' or the Extreme Left. The constitutionalists, at least, knew what they were doing.

8

The Authorities

EACH STUDENT disturbance in the two years 1968–70 brought complaints from the public about the inactivity of the authorities. 'Why don't the authorities do something?' was a question normally linked with 'Why don't the moderates do something?' The 'something' that such questioners wanted carried out was the expulsion of the disrupters. The authorities were the targets of much criticism for not expelling the disrupters.

One of the difficulties and yet a necessary step in answering this question is that of defining the 'authorities'. Universities are not ruled by despotic vice-chancellors. The 'authorities' differed from place to place in where power lay. At Warwick power was ultimately in the hands of the council which had a majority of lay members. At the L.S.E. it was in the hands of the court of governors in which Lord Robbins, the chairman, had a deciding voice. At other institutions the senior staff exercised a decisive influence. At Bradford and a few other institutions students were on the policy-making bodies. The authorities of any institution covered an amorphous mass of people in which actual power was often exercised by the most energetic and persistent. Divisions among the 'authorities' of any college were as marked as those among the students. To discipline students vice-chancellors and principals had to have not only the complicit apathy of the student bodies but also the support of a large proportion of their staffs and the approval of any external bodies with power over the institutions. To these obvious difficulties were added the division of the staff into academic and administrative sections. This had been made inevitable by university expansion.

Thus each vice-chancellor was subject to pressures from his staff.

Nor could he necessarily expect support from his colleagues. The committee of vice-chancellors included men of very varied attitudes to disruption. Mr. James Drever, vice-chancellor of Dundee University, seemed prepared to condone the offences of those who wished to prevent Mr. Powell from giving a speech at the university. On the other hand Professor Roderick Collar of Bristol University and Sir William Mansfield Cooper of Manchester University were hard-line opponents of disruption and immediately took legal action when it threatened their institutions. Dr. Sloman of Essex University was perhaps the most 'liberal'. In May 1969 he said, 'I want to proclaim the right of students to dissent and show them no area is sacrosanct.' Two months earlier he had admitted that all was not well. 'If you have a system where students are free then you will have a minority of students who will abuse this system . . . you have got to believe in the good sense, co-operation and loyalty of the majority. What we are now attempting to do better is in dealing effectively with the minority who will abuse a system of this kind.' He said that student activities had never disrupted the working of the university. In the autumn of 1969 the working of the university was disrupted. In December Dr. Sloman said, 'We have to succeed in reconciling the passionate idealism of our younger members, their questioning of accepted opinion and their enormous energy with tolerance for the opinions of others and respect for order.' Dr. Sloman was nothing if not consistent. Others were less consistent. Professor Briggs of Sussex in January 1969 uncompromisingly opposed an occupation of the administration block on behalf of L.S.E. students. The following year he did not oppose or punish the disrupters of the Files Controversy. At Birmingham Dr. Brockie Hunter took first the hard line and then the soft line to end the 1968 occupation.

Each staff was as varied as the committee of vice-chancellors. At Birmingham the opinion of some staff was expressed by Mr. David Leigh, assistant to the administrator of the halls of residence. 'We have been chucked out of the administration building, and I wish to protest in the strongest possible terms about the way in which the university authorities have allowed a minority of students to take over this department of the university.' Another section of the staff took a different view. 'The vast majority of the students have, in fact, behaved with great dignity.' This band of opinion was perhaps best represented by the theology lecturer who sent a message of goodwill and an injunction to reconciliation to all. On the Extreme Left a social studies lecturer defended the sitters-in and their 'able and eloquent speeches'. It is hardly surprising that Dr. Brockie Hunter found firmness difficult. The distribution of opinion was made clear the following year when the staff over-whelmingly refused to support the application for a permanent post by a sociology lecturer who had helped to lead the occupation. The local branch of the Association of University Teachers stated there was no reason to suspect political rather than academic reasons for his rejection. The same hard-line opposition to disruption was shown by most of the staff of Kent in 1970. The constitutionalists formed a far higher portion of the staff than of the students at nearly all institutions. Moreover, under pressure 'moderates' on the staff tended to turn to constitutionalism. This happened at L.S.E. where the disruption of lectures in 1969 drove the staff to support the governors in disciplining disrupters. At L.S.E. there was an unusually large proportion of staff led by the Professor of English Law which was prepared to vote against discipline for disruption once it had taken place. The staff ranged from Dr. Devletoglou who believed in the firmest possible action to the dismissed sociology lecturer who believed in the widest possible disruption. In between were those like Professor Mackenzie who advocated enquiries and compromises. However, as mentioned above, the staff line hardened. Unlike the students the staff were not muddle-headed enough to vote against discipline if the motion to this effect contained a clause condemning disruption as well. L.S.E. also provided an example of the distribution of opinion by department. The staff of the international history department were hard-core opponents of disruption. The staff of the sociology department inclined to the Left and the Extreme Left. This was perhaps even more obvious at Birmingham where the staff of the sociology department were almost the only ones who wanted to see the applicant of the Extreme Left appointed. At one institution, however, the staff in effect condoned disruption. This was Warwick where the staff joined in the wave of criticism. It is hardly surprising that the senate decided to take no disci-plinary action. It must be said that most staff showed little consistent interest in university politics. Their teaching and research left them little time. This was particularly true of science and the exact arts. Teachers of these subjects tended to be more opposed to disruption.

The basic difficulty confronting the authorities when coherent and agreed policies were being evolved was that of facing the fact that one cannot be liberal all the time. Vice-chancellors and staffs sometimes seemed to feel guilty about criticizing their charges and face-saving formulas were produced to conceal the pointlessness of disruption. At Swansea in February 1970 dozens of the staff signed a letter sympathizing with students on strike and eventually the strike was stopped with the aid of a statement to the effect that there might have been a misunderstanding. This 'misunderstanding' formula was used by some university authorities in the Files Controversy. Some principals seemed to feel diffident about attacking the Extreme Left or even the N.U.S. unless they attacked the Right also. Condemning Mr. Jack Straw's refusal explicitly to uphold Mr. Powell's right to speak Lord Annan, the provost of University College, London, described Mr. Powell as a 'whey-faced fanatic'. His view was more clearly expressed, however, than that of Mr. Drever of Dundee whose attitude towards potential disruptions of Mr. Powell's projected visit was at best ambiguous. L.S.E. authorities postponed as long as they could facing the fact that there were some staff and students determined not to tolerate the institution. In November 1968 the governors announced that the immaturity of the lecturers involved in the recent occupation protected them from discipline unless they erred again. The following term they erred again and this time conflict was inevitable. Some authorities did not seem to realize the implications of their own actions. When Professor Briggs, vice-chancellor of Sussex University, refused to take any notice of the exclusion of the Right-winger, Sir Archibald James, from the university premises he made it inevitable that this erosion of freedom of speech would eventually extend, when students felt like extending it, to the disruption of lectures. When Sir Archibald James approached the university he was confronted by a crowd of students and a university official suggested that he should leave at once. This was symbolic of the attitude of some authorities. A similar incident occurred at Essex University when a reporter was punched by a student. Other students stood round, disapproving but inactive. A university official came and advised the reporter to leave. There was in many cases a reluctance to face trouble. After the November 1968 disruption of Major Wall's speech at York, the vice-chancellor, Lord James, had talks with the president of the union about how to prevent the repetition of such outbreaks. He did not seem to consider the possibility that such outbreaks might be inevitable from such people. Professor Harry Rée of the same institution said that in future York facilities would not be made available to speakers whose visits could arouse understandable opposition. The firmest line had been taken the previous month by a staff-student working party. 'Those members of a university, whether staff or student, who accept neither learning as the primary and over-riding purpose of a university nor the need to vest some authority in a qualified teaching staff, should, if they are honest, seek their livelihood in other kinds of educational institution—or none.' It did not suggest methods of preventing the state of affairs it feared. A similar fear of being illiberal affected individual teachers in institutions. When told that one of his new students had been a member of the Schools Action Union a Sussex tutor said, 'Good, we want a few students who can think for themselves.' It did not seem to occur to him that membership of S.A.U. was not necessarily indicative of independence of mind. In some quarters it was considered liberal to be uncritical of the Extreme Left at least hesitant about dealing with disruption.

Not only the fear of being illiberal but that of admitting that the selection process was inefficient affected the authorities. It was difficult for the authorities to denounce the disruptive minorities wholeheartedly when they had been responsible for admitting them. This was particularly true of L.S.E. where Lord Robbins had led the movement for university expansion and the inclusion of as large a proportion of the population in universities as possible. He could obviously not attribute disruption to the inadequacies of his students. Many university authorities showed a desire to be on the side of their students and to believe that their choice had been justified.

Also there were occasions on which university authorities found it difficult to take the activities of their students seriously. The

Keele nude sun-bathing incident provides an instance of this. A university spokesman found the students' behaviour unimportant but there was an avalanche of complaints from the public. At length token fines were imposed.

Thus over the whole two years there was paralysing division and confusion among those responsible for keeping order in universities. It is some measure of the indecision of the authorities that at Sussex and Bradford student representation on policy-making bodies was increased after the unions had made clear that they had no sympathy with the defence of the right of unpopular speakers to speak. It was as difficult morally as it was physically for the authorities to act. These two years saw the polarization of university teachers. One was headed by the Professor of English Law at the L.S.E. and took a lenient view of disruption. The other was headed by Professor Cox of Manchester and it believed in the punishment of disruption. It contained supporters of all political sympathies of the liberal democratic kind. What made the task of the hard-line staff more difficult was its opposition to governmental intervention in university affairs. Some of the constitutionalist staff were opposing not only the demands of student revelation but those of government utilitarianism. The constitutionalist staff were also opposed to the wish of some of the public to have students expelled for reasons irrelevant to university life. They were indeed pressed.

It was frequently suggested that university authorities should use some sort of force. Private police forces were suggested for the special use of universities. Most people in universities were horrified by this prospect. It was also frequently suggested that the ordinary police should be called in. The vice-chancellors of even the most disturbed institutions, such as L.S.E. and Birmingham, considered this the last resort. Dr. Adams of L.S.E. considered it almost indecent. This did not prevent him from calling the police in to close the L.S.E. and protect it from the attempts of the Extreme Left to recapture it. The police complained that the three weeks' guarding L.S.E. had been an expensive waste of manpower and made it clear that they were unwilling to intervene and stop further occupations. At Bristol a similar problem arose and after the sit-in the Watch Committee considered the possibility of giving wider powers and responsibilities to the police. The difficulty was that there was a gap sanctified by law and custom in the enforcement of order in universities. It had always been a tradition that petty crimes committed by students, especially on university premises, had not received the full attention of the police but had been left for the authorities to deal with. This had worked while each academic community had felt a corporate responsibility and had a common set of values. Once students repudiated the obligations towards their colleges that had previously protected them to some extent from the full operation of the law they were in fact subject to little physical restraint. Disruption could continue unchecked until students tired of it. All that the authorities could do was to take legal action for particular disturbances against a few identifiable students. Such legal proceedings took time. The American revolutionary student most energetically involved in the 1968–69 L.S.E. commotions was not imprisoned for breaking the subsequent legal injunctions until April 1970.

This vacuum of jurisdiction coincided with the introduction of anomalies into the laws governing responsibility of those exactly within the undergraduate age-range of 18–21. Parliament lowered the age of majority from 21 to 18. The universities were no longer *in loco parentis*. Almost all their students were legally adult in most respects. However when they came before the courts their youth ensured that the traditional penalties for minors rather than for adults were incurred. The law indeed provided many complications for vice-chancellors who tried to exercise some control over their students. Sir James Tait, vice-chancellor of the City University, London, once considered sueing the university's magazine, *Beacon*, for libelling him. However, according to the university's charter, the vice-chancellor was ultimately responsible.

In the circumstances the university authorities did what they could. Student disturbances had made them produce elaborate disciplinary processes with many safeguards for student rights of appeal. These had originally been instituted to forestall accusations that students were disciplined hastily and arbitrarily. The result was that disciplinary proceedings took so long that sentences were normally announced in the summer term when disruption had lost its supporters and its vitality. Thus those disciplined received little assistance from their colleagues. It was this humiliation rather

than the sentences themselves that gave the sentences such deter-
rent value as they had.

Thus the university authorities acted as they did because they
were divided in every possible way and subject to every possible
pressure, including moral blackmail from students and financial
blackmail from local authorities. Whatever they did or did not do
they were criticized both inside and outside their institutions by
both the progressive and the traditional. They were unable to
reconcile their desire to be liberal with their duty to keep order.

The saddest comment was made by Mr. Alesdair MacIntyre,
former Dean of Students at Essex: 'Ironically our mistake was to
be so liberal. If only we'd started the university with a mass of
restrictive rules, the students would have spent their time happily
breaking rule after rule. As it is we gave them near-Utopia, they
have no real practical injustices to fight against, so they had to
rebel on ideological issues like germ warfare and Vietnam; and
these we are powerless to alter.'

9

The Press and Public Opinion

IT HAS often been asserted that university disturbances have been much exaggerated by the Press and Television, that such exaggeration has inflamed public opinion and that the Press has contributed to the polarization of sympathies. Such assertions are only partly justified.

The Press reflected rather than inflamed public opinion and it was, indeed, kinder to the Extreme Left than were most of the public. It may not have been entirely truthful but it was, in a factual sense, largely accurate. The events it described did occur; and if the camera can show lies it does not lie. Perhaps the worst fault of the Press was to take student commotions seriously in the wrong way. The space devoted to student disturbances was made possible by the relative placidity of life in this country.

Over the two years 1968–70 the attitude of the Press changed. The expectation and even the hope of what was emphasized as 'firm action' began to fade and it began to be assumed that if students were so consistently troublesome—and both Press and public believed wrongly that they were consistently troublesome— they must have something to be troublesome about. Disapproval withered into indifference and indifference into partial condonation. The condemnation by the Press of the break-ins in the Files Controversy in 1970 was much more half-hearted than the condemnation of the occupations of 1968. It is doubtful whether the attitude of the public was modified as much as was that of the Press. It can safely be asserted that public opinion was, as a whole, opposed to student disruption.

There was considerable variety of opinion in the Press. The *Guardian* published such articles as 'Are our universities fit for students?' The *News of the World* asked, 'Are we getting our money's worth out of students?' On the whole *The Times* and the *Guardian* showed the widest spread of views within their columns, particularly in the correspondence sections. There was less division among the readers of the *Daily Sketch*. Except in the *Guardian*, *New Society*, the *Morning Star* and *New Statesman* the overwhelming majority of letters, articles and leaders were, to put it mildly, critical of student disrupters. Broadly speaking, attitudes could be divided into three types. One group maintained that disrupters should be sent down. One group claimed that the disrupters were idealists who went too far sometimes. One group believed that the disrupters were totally justified. These groups have been listed in decreasing order of size.

The tone of *The Times* is difficult to describe because its leaders tended to take the disrupters less seriously than did the specialist educational articles. Its leader on the L.S.E. gates was headed 'Nor Iron Bars a Cage'. Its specialist educational articles contained such assessments as, 'They are a new breed, feeling international bonds with the young everywhere, openly seeking a new approach to life.' The tone of most of the letters is suggested by such headings as, 'Send them down', though a substantial minority maintained that disruption was not entirely the fault of students. Of the L.S.E. disrupters Professor Crick of Sheffield University wrote in: 'Those who assaulted members of the staff or fellow-students and who broke up lectures should go but so should those who failed to prevent this mess.' This view that acts of violence were not necessarily the responsibility of those who committed them was as already stated shared at first by Mr. Ian Taylor of the F.C.S. 'The university council, by refusing to listen to moderate demands, have forced students to take direct action.' On the same day as this defence of the Birmingham occupation *The Times* leader was 'Time for Discipline' and the correspondence columns contained a letter demanding the expulsion of disrupters who were wasting the taxpayers' money. This was a favourite theme of letters denouncing disruption, though it was slightly less frequently hammered home in *The Times*, the *Guardian* and the *Telegraph* than it was in some other papers.

The *Telegraph*, both the *Daily* and the *Sunday* varieties, and the *Guardian* represented the more articulate Right and Left respectively. Editorials in the *Telegraph* had such headings as 'Ineffectual Dons'. Editorials in the *Guardian* had such headings as 'Effectual Dons'. The cancellation of the South African cricket tour was greeted with a leader entitled 'Let Violence Celebrate' in the *Telegraph* and 'The Right Decision at Last' in the *Guardian*. Nearly all the letters in the *Telegraph* were opposed to university disruption. Those in the *Guardian* were divided. It was the usual channel of criticism of authority. Dismissed Hornsey staff wrote in: '. . . Long and patient campaign of persecution . . . All we need right now is one more letter from the whelkstall governors, justifying their capacity and ill-will in that bureaucratic treacle-language that has become so familiar to us and *Guardian* readers.' The suggestion in *Guardian* leaders that students went too far sometimes brought in angry letters. The *Guardian* illustrated the dilemma of progressive liberals. Its editorials, articles and correspondence columns showed a strong desire to avoid at all costs the label of 'Right-wing'. Behaviour realized to be 'boorish exhibitionism' was often criticized less because it was wrong than because it might provoke a backlash; this diminished the guilt felt at condemning student disrupters. While some of the reporters of the *Telegraph* maintained that disturbances were not caused by lack of participation, some of those of the *Guardian* maintained that they were. It is fair to say that to judge from the correspondence columns a proportion of the readers of the *Telegraph* believed in the Great Red Plot and a similar proportion of the *Guardian* readers believed in the Great Establishment Conspiracy. The *Guardian*'s response to student unrest was that a change in the nature and purpose of universities should be seriously considered. It attributed the violence committed at and planned for sports matches between British and South African teams to racial segregation in South Africa and suggested that police and stewards might be 'tactless'. However it opposed the official photographing of violent episodes and those involved. On the Files Controversy its attitude was clear. It condemned the theft of confidential documents and published excerpts from them. It would be reasonable to conclude that its general view was somewhere between the 'moderates' and the constitutionalists of the university world. However it printed letters of all types. Many letters were published condemning disruption and a far smaller proportion of these than in any other paper took the taxpayers' money as their theme.

The *Sunday Times* and the *Observer* were harder-line liberal papers. As a *Sunday Times* leader put it, 'This newspaper vigorously opposes those views [of Mr. Powell]. But it equally vigorously asserts the right of Mr. Powell or anyone else to be heard.' However, the usual fear of reaction came through: 'Much of the student unrest, in this country and abroad, springs from genuine causes and is worthy of genuine sympathy.' The *Observer*'s attitude was similar. Of the weekly magazines the *New Statesman* was somewhere to the Left of the *Guardian*. The sentiments expressed varied from 'The new movement has proved its political significance . . . Almost all the marchers were young and most seemed to be students or friends of students . . . This is the New Model Army of revolutionary puritanism: stern, purposeful, doctrinaire, uncompromising, contemptuous of people like Mervyn Jones. And 20,000 of them!' to 'Most of the crowd reaction I observed was bored and cynical . . . Even among the "respectable" marchers, I saw some make ugly attempts to provoke the police.' These were observations on the Great Vietnam March. The *Spectator*'s attitude to the March was simpler; its leader was headed 'Enter the New Fascists'. However it did not wish to seem entirely lacking in progressive feeling and when the L.S.E. was closed described the governors of L.S.E. as the Grand Old Dukes of York. It is worth noting that a don under the pseudonym of 'Ian MacGregor' forecast, in three articles in the *Spectator* in the autumn of 1968, the course of events over the next few years.

The danger is that, through a natural (if timid) reluctance to utter certain home-truths, the universities will allow themselves to be morally blackmailed into accepting changes which they do not desire and which could, in the not so long run, destroy morale among university teachers and cause British academic standards to decline sharply . . . The great majority of students, anxious to lead normal lives and finding the strident tone of university politics increasingly distasteful, lapse into apathy; they play no part in student affairs. But at the same time this same apathetic majority becomes steadily more convinced of the legitimacy of the militants' demands.

He actually suggested that most students were less intelligent and hard-working than most dons.

The *Morning Star*'s editorials, articles and letters were in a sense consistent. They claimed that the decadence of Western society drove students into commotions but that students were wrong to condemn the East European states as no better and as capitalist, imperialist and bureaucratic. A typical article was headed 'How Universities are Shaped to serve Capitalism' and began, 'Learning is perhaps man's greatest pleasure'. It supported university revolutionaries only up to a point and in fear of the Right-wing backlash did not encourage uncritically. The best-known communist student, who sometimes wrote in the *Morning Star* in fact was opposed to violence in the Files Controversy. Like the rest of the Press, including the *Guardian* and the *New Statesman*, the *Morning Star* was considered a mouthpiece of conservatism not to say reaction, by the Extreme Left.

These papers both reflected and informed opinion. A sufficiently large proportion of the readers had enough independence of mind for it to be possible to talk of articulate public opinion. The readers of these papers constituted a minority of the population. In 1968 the circulation of *The Times* was 400,000, of the *Daily Telegraph* 1,407,000, of the *Guardian* 281,000, of the *Sunday Times* 1,461,000, of the *Observer*, 903,000, of the *Sunday Telegraph* 713,000, of the *New Statesman*, about 100,000 and of the *Spectator* about 30,000. No figures are available for the circulation of the *Morning Star*.

The other group of papers had a larger and less critical readership. Its readers often did not realize that the paper of their choice was sometimes biased and selective. These papers moulded opinion and directed anger much more than the former group did.

The view of the *Daily Express* and the *Sunday Express* was clear and consistent. 'They want to fail five times' was the heading of a *Daily Express* article on the law school sit-in of November 1968. Leaders in the *Sunday Express* included 'End this Menace'. This called for the exclusion of foreign agitators. 'Deport them, soak them, cut their grants', was the headline on October 27, 1968. It was a paraphrase of Sir Gerald Nabarro's speech on the subject. There was a strong belief that foreign agitators were causing much if not most of the trouble. Correspondence columns had headings such as 'Those bobbies were too soft on the thugs'. One of the few leaders commending any action of the Labour Prime Minister, Mr. Harold Wilson, was one headed 'The Right Decision', on Mr. Wilson's refusal to consider the suggestion that students should play a part in assessing staff bonuses. Even the *Express*, however, occasionally yielded to the wish not to appear too Right-wing. It described L.S.E. governors as 'hamfisted'. In 1968 the circulation of the *Daily Express* was 3,853,000 and of the *Sunday Express*, 4,238,000.

The *Daily Mirror*, circulation 5,034,000, had a readership of similar views on student unrest. The leaders were less entirely critical of it. Its news items on disturbances presented them in a simple light. The report of the L.S.E. Oration Day disruption of December 1969 was particularly vivid. The disrupters were denounced as Red Fascists. Most of the readers' letters on student disturbances were hostile.

The *Daily Mail*'s editorials, letters and articles were also hostile. A typical article was headed 'The Wild Ones'. Its circulation was 2,095,000.

The most extreme views in the daily papers appeared in the *Daily Sketch*, circulation 915,000. Articles had headings like 'How REAL is the threat of an October revolt'. Letters included such sentiments as 'The whole march stinks of being communist-inspired' and 'How can white students burn the Union Jack and support Black Power? Has the country gone off its head?' One letter suggested closing the universities for five years.

This line was taken also by the *News of the World*, circulation 6,191,000. In October 1968 it ran a series, 'The Great Student Plot'. Of revolutionary students it alleged, 'They are part of a giant international conspiracy to disrupt and embarrass Britain, America and the other Western allies.' It was alleged that the plot was organized at Bayonne in France and referred to hundreds of foreign agitators lurking in the L.S.E. for the Great Vietnam March. The *News of the World* was taken more seriously by its readers than in universities. The president of Keele students' union wrote in that his institution had not been placed high enough in the league-table of disturbed universities.

The *People*, circulation 5,533,000, was unfriendly to disruption. Both the *People* and the *News of the World* sometimes gave the impression that universities were dens of sexual vice. If they had been there might have been less political disturbance. A Family Planning Association survey suggested that students were more restrained than their working contemporaries. Venereal disease was rarer than in the general population. It is fair to say that the greater a paper's circulation and the lower the social classes for which it catered the more irrelevant and factually inaccurate were its reports. The sensational episodes were given more importance than the real issues.

The local papers were slightly different. They reflected local opinion immediately. By some of the public any restraint was viewed as softness. Some papers showed little restraint. The *Western Evening Press* covered the 1968 Bristol sit-in and included such headings as 'Reds Back Them' and 'More Like a Love-in than a Sit-in'. Leaders had such headings as 'Get the Rebels OUT'. Nearly all the letters in this paper and in another local paper, the *Evening Post*, were hostile to the sitters-in. The *Birmingham Post* and the *Birmingham Evening Mail* were on their university's sit-in less whole-hearted and less ill-informed and were for these reasons attacked in the correspondence columns. People wrote in demanding the return of national service. The few approving the winds of change were swamped. The best students could hope for was the indifference suggested by a survey conducted by the *Yorkshire Evening Post*. A few local papers were favourable. It was possible to read the *Eastern Evening News* account of Mr. Roy Jenkins's visit to the University of East Anglia without realizing that he had been shouted down. The correspondence columns were less kind. They referred to 'the yobs who chanted, parrot-like, their second-hand slogans'. Many of the letters in local papers on the disruption of meetings addressed by Right-wing M.P.s suggested that their authors were moved less by love of freedom of speech than by sympathy with the views of those shouted down. This was particularly true of reactions to the disruption of Mr. Powell's speeches.

It must be stated that the 'revolutionaries' were wrong in asserting that the Press was deliberately mendacious, and misleading and wrong in asserting that the Press was entirely against them. Almost every paper and periodical, from *The Times* to the smallest local paper, printed letters and articles by the Extreme Left. The result was in nearly every case a flood of indignant letters. The Extreme Left's reaction to this indignation was to assert that public opinion had been so conditioned and corrupted that it could not recognize the truth when the truth was put before it.

Strongly as people often felt about student disruption in general they felt even more strongly about it when it occurred in their localities. The people of Colchester, Cambridge, Brighton and London felt particularly strongly. In November 1968 Mr. David Brooker, a Colchester businessman, urged his colleagues to join him in withdrawing support from Essex University. In February 1969 Mr. Cecil Howe, mayor of Colchester, said that the behaviour of some Essex students had aroused widespread concern and that there should be more discipline. Mr. James Wentworth Day, an author living locally, was franker. 'Its [Essex's] record of hooliganism and violence is appalling. Most responsible people in Essex regard it as a blot on the county.' The following year there were stormy discussions in the county council about whether the grant to the university should be cut. At Cambridge the mayor and the council demanded condign punishment for the Garden House disrupters. The sentences meted out received their approval. At Brighton a long series of incidents, including disruption of a council meeting by Sussex undergraduates and the exclusion of a local Right-wing notable from the university premises, resulted in the council's carrying a proposal for the withdrawal of grants from misbehaving undergraduates. The cutting of the local grant to Sussex University was also considered. The London School of Economics was the target of much criticism in the *Evening Standard* and the *Evening News*. It was widely known in the neighbourhood as the London School for Bleeding Comics.

There was a belief shared by the authorities of Sussex and Essex, and to some extent of L.S.E., that improved public relations would help their local and national images of their institutions. There was a refusal to admit that student unpopularity was due to student misbehaviour and not to misunderstanding. These efforts at improving the reputations of these universities were completely unsuccessful.

Normally the organ for public disapproval was the council. Councils all over the country tried to use their financial power. In the autumn of 1968 the councils of West Bromwich, Birmingham,

Warley and Lytham St. Anne's tried to exercise power in this way. In March 1970 Liverpool council followed suit. A few months later Keele was subjected to the same pressure. The councils were in their turn hard pressed by public opinion. This was most clearly seen in Birmingham where contributions to the university's Rag Week fell from about £12,500 to about £3,000.

The involvement of local authorities, particularly in the case of art colleges which were under their control, meant the intrusion of party politics. The Liberal parliamentary candidate for Guildford used the situation there to embarrass the Conservative council. Although Labour and Liberal voters were almost as opposed to student disruption as were Conservative voters the party leaders were split. The meetings of the Birmingham sit-in were chaired by a local Labour parliamentary candidate while the Labour minority on the council denounced the sit-in. Local councils were more closely connected with their districts than were M.P.s and candidates. However through division and confusion public opinion made itself felt at local level more vigorously than at national level.

On some matters public opinion asserted itself vigorously at national level. One of these matters was the 1968 proposal that students should help to assess lecturers' bonuses. The wrath of the lecturers was exceeded by the wrath of the public; many seemed to feel that such assessment of financial worth might more properly be done by the teachers of the taught. The view of the Essex student who said, 'The country needs our talents. If we strike they have to listen,' was not widely shared. Another matter on which the public expressed itself vigorously was what became known as the Students' Mistresses Controversy of 1970. This proposal, involving fewer than a dozen students a year, was an administrative adjustment transferring responsibility for financial allowances for those ladies living with students from one government department to another. The House of Lords at first refused to sanction this transference which had, publicized in lurid form by the tabloids, raised a public outcry. These two episodes illustrated the weakness of public opposition to disruption in universities. It sometimes concentrated on the wrong issues or the right issues for the wrong reasons. It was of dubious value to the constitutionalists and the authorities within universities. When it concentrated on the right issues for the right reasons such as freedom of speech, staff control over academic matters or staff freedom from financial pressure from students, it was weakened by its reputation in universities for susceptibility to the Great Red Plot and Dens of Vice and Drugs theories.

Some pressure groups in decline attempted to tap what they believed to be the vitality of student protest. The Liberal Party and the churches were the best examples of this. In a pamphlet published in the summer of 1969 the British Council of Churches claimed that such protest was at its best a desire to return to the medieval community of scholars. The Liberal Party, or rather some of its leading members, took the view that the disrupters were to some extent rendered less blameworthy by their progressive intentions. Organizations with greater followings and more coherent opinions were less inclined to risk what they had in order to seem progressive. This was true of the Catholic Church and the Conservative Party.

Over the two years 1968–70 public opinion and the Press were and remained hostile to disruption in universities. But to some extent the heart went out of the articulate opposition. By July 1970 student disturbances had become so condoned by the immunity of custom that much of the Press seemed shocked by the sentences imposed on the Garden House rioters. Some papers had already had their confidence in opposing disruption shaken. Having in December 1968 demanded 'firm action' against the Birmingham sitters-in the *Birmingham Post* in March 1970 published, despite legal injunctions, material stolen by Warwick students from the university authorities.

While one section of opinion hardened another softened. Some held to the view expressed in a letter to the *News of the World*.

Too many second-class students still think we are a lot of illiterate peasants who regard them as leaders who will take us into a revolution whenever they think fit.

Another view was put in a letter to the *Daily Mirror*.

Do we middle-aged people honestly expect the youth of today to respect our generation after the unholy mess we have made of things over the past twenty years? I feel sorry for the young folk who have to face a future of hire purchase, housing shortage, the threat of war and a society where self-interest is its main morality. Anything youth can suggest must be an improvement on the degraded mentality of our generation.

The same view was expressed by a *Times* education correspondent.

Yet the most profound question is why so many of the most able and articulate students of their generation no longer uphold the values of British life.

He did not give any indication of what he meant by 'many', 'able' or 'articulate'. The same view was also expressed in the *Guardian*.

. . . some of the most able and impatient men and women of their generation who are quite rightly ardent for change, in the university and in society at large.

An unhealthy spirit of irrational self-flagellation began to take articulate expression. It began to be assumed that if the traditional bases of universities were being attacked there must necessarily be something wrong with them and with the liberal society and the parliamentary system within which they flourished. It was held that if the attacks were being made by 'the young' they were more justifiable and more deserving of surrender. The urge not to appear reactionary—every paper warned against the backlash without admitting to being part of it—resulted in lack of confidence in any set of values.

Thus the Press and public opinion though still overwhelmingly hostile to university disruption found their opposition both worn down and undermined. The section inclined to concede gained passive adherents if not active supporters. It must be stated that the disrupters were encouraged by the attention they received from the Press, the public and T.V. T.V., indeed, had more immediate but less lasting impact than the Press as it had, for reasons of time, to pack all the issues together in a sensational and simple form. The Press and public opinion were, like the constitutionalists, the 'moderates' and the authorities, worn down.

IO

The Disrupters

THE QUESTION naturally arises, 'What are the disrupters like?'
This is most frequently asked after some violent and much
publicized incident. People wonder about the characters and
motives of those involved. It is usually accounts, films and record-
ings of riots or disruptions of political meetings that arouse the
most horrified curiosity in the public.

It is easiest to begin by stating what the disrupters were not.
They were not, despite assertions in *Time and Tide*, organized by
the Kremlin. No evidence whatsoever has been produced to support the Great Red Plot theory. When asked for such evidence
those contending that there is a Great Red Plot say stubbornly
only that they 'know' that there is one. There was no sinister
organization behind the wide variety of commotions. The fluctua-
tion in numbers involved make such a view almost untenable.

The disrupter despised the Russian type of communism and the
Maoism of the Maoists was an abstract belief unconnected with
China as she is. University disruption was unaffected by world
politics or foreign countries. The October 27, 1968 Vietnam March
sank into student-lore and practical oblivion. The moratorium
called in America a year later to impress the President with the
strength of feeling on Vietnam attracted few imitators in Britain.
In L.S.E. the Extreme Left had, as recorded earlier, to hold their
meetings on the Moratorium in the bar to have an audience. The
shooting of four students in America the following May in a
demonstration about the extension into Cambodia of the Vietnam
War aroused little reaction in Britain. The Vietnam War had
outlived its excitement value. World political events were the
occasion and not the cause of disturbance in Britain.

Disrupters were not paid by foreign agents. Disruptive groups received their money from subsidies paid by members and from such sources as collections and dances. Their sources of income were as unblameworthy as those of any Conservative Association—except for sums voted for individuals by packed union meetings and interviews sold by disrupters to the Press. It was not the sources of income but the ways in which it was spent that caused trouble. There were wrangles about how it should be spent and which group of 'revolutionaries' should receive most. 'Red Gold', however, was a myth.

Another myth connected with this is the belief that foreign students were responsible for much or most of the commotions. With very few exceptions most of the disrupters have been British. Most of the few foreign disrupters were American. At L.S.E. the American disrupters did not see eye-to-eye with the British disrupters. National differences made themselves felt; visiting Americans and others were often the most extreme, since they had to pack their revolution into their one year overseas.

These were the most famous myths firmly believed in by many of the overwhelming majority opposed to disruption. Those who held that the disrupters had some grievances or were good lads who went a little far sometimes believed in a different set of myths. These took away some of the guilt felt at opposing or criticizing any group describing itself as Left-wing and progressive. One of these myths is that the disrupters were the most able students. Examination results do not substantiate this belief. The leaflets put out by the Extreme Left were alarmingly semi-literate. The distribution of intelligence in the different bands of university opinion can best be illustrated by the fact that a larger proportion of undergraduates than of post-graduates were disrupters and that a larger proportion of postgraduates than of staff were disrupters. It is also necessary to dispel the illusion that the disrupters were the most articulate section of student opinion. There is nothing articulate about screaming 'fascist pig!'—especially when the screamer cannot, when challenged, define fascism. Nor is it true that the Extreme Left was in any real sense democratic, egalitarian and anxious to secure equal participation in university and government for all. Of every 200 disrupters only about 20 addressed meetings and formulated policy. This hard core was usually divided on doctrinal issues. The other 180 played the role of a chorus. This meant that they did not feel responsible for carrying out proposals for which they voted. The leaders of the Extreme Left never believed that all students had equal political rights or judgement. When the Birmingham students' guild voted against continuing the occupation the president said that this majority

> had not applied enough thought to the question of the sit-in. To ask people to go to the meeting and judge, when only aware of public opinion through the kind of press publicity we have had is asking too much of even the most intelligent engineer. . . . For the first time students have some kind of power and we ought to recognize this.

When it was pointed out to the sitters-in at the Inns of Court that their actions had been disowned by the majority of their colleagues they maintained that they were 'the representatives of the real interests of the majority of students'. The Extreme Left always believed that it had a duty to 'educate' its own outer core and the other students.

It is not true that the Extreme Left was seeking freedom of speech. In so far as freedom of any sort was involved the Extreme Left has been seeking freedom of action to shut other people up. It is not true that the Extreme Left was trying to lead 'the working class' to the barricades. It made token attempts to contact 'the working class' but would have been nonplussed if thousands of miners, shop assistants and dockers had marched to the university strongholds demanding immediate revolution. The Extreme Left may have wanted to feel revolutionary but it did not actually want revolution. It was well aware of the immense hostility aroused by its activities but made no effort to improve its image or manipulate public opinion by even a little self-restraint. Although aware that riots were self-defeating in terms of revolutionary feeling it continued in them. It protected itself from knowledge of popular feeling and maintained its illusion of 'the working class' by meeting, at most, untypical politically-minded members of 'the working class'. The 'revolutionaries' did not usually go to London dockers and harangue them on the evils of racialism. In this way they kept their idealized image of 'the working class' pure. The posters of the Extreme Left portrayed 'the working class' as it was in 1920. There was no realization that the horny-handed sons of toil form a much smaller proportion of the total labour force than they did.

Nor is it true that the Extreme Left was moved by intellectual curiosity or a desire for dialogue and discussion. 'We as questioners are forced to take action to get our views heard' is how one 'revolutionary' put it. Shouting down was a method of avoiding discussion or debate. If the Extreme Left has no real beliefs it has also no doubts. Thus the spirit of criticism and debate never developed. Persuasion and exposition were as little considered as the empirically verifiable facts. This is most clearly illustrated by the receptions given to Mr. Powell. Mr. Powell's allegations about immigrants could be, and often were, empirically disproved in debate. None of these debates took place in universities where students preferred the self-indulgence of shouting him down, thus achieving for him the maximum publicity.

Nor is it true that the Extreme Left was honourable. The mendacity of its publications gave rise to threats of libel action. Since such publications were not signed such threats were difficult to carry out. Many of their attacks were personally venomous. When Dr. Adams was made director of L.S.E. the Socialist Society published a leaflet attacking his wife. One virtue not shown by the Extreme Left was courage. The overwhelming majority did not have the courage to address a friendly meeting, let alone a hostile one. The leaders provoked the authorities to discipline them, refused to accept punishment and restraint and appealed to their colleagues for protection. They wanted martyrdom and complained when it was more expensive than they expected. In so far as the Files Controversy had any significance it was about whether students should be held responsible for their own actions. It did not affect most of the Extreme Left for they did not become known individually but those who proposed and carried out acts of violence amid great publicity objected to having actions which they believed to be right recorded for future assessment of them. Most of those who voted for occupations were not sufficiently committed to spend the night on a cold hard floor. Revolution in universities in most cases stopped for vacations, Sundays, examinations and the last bus home. The Extreme Left did not have the courage of its convictions. To describe it as honourable or sincere is to strain the meanings of these adjectives.

It is not true that the Extreme Left was trying to improve the position in society of underprivileged groups. It agitated about the treatment of immigrants and women. The Springboks riots, however, can scarcely have contributed to racial harmony in Britain. The N.U.S. was, as a Labour M.P., Mr. Christopher Price, said, largely a male organization. The further Left student groups were the more unusual it was for a woman member to address a meeting or help to formulate policy. The division of labour followed traditional lines. Warwick had a lady vice-president to deal with problems women are supposed to be particularly equipped to deal with. At York gipsy children 'adopted' by students were as stated earlier looked after by women students. Only Sussex and L.S.E. Extreme Left produced any well-known hard-line articulate women activists. Even allowing for the fact that there are three men undergraduates to every woman undergraduate 'revolution' had a surprisingly masculine leadership. At L.S.E. only one woman revolutionary frequently addressed meetings. The activities of the rest of the women of the Extreme Left were confined to greeting constitutionalist men speakers with ovations of hissing. As a complement to this the masculine chorus of the Extreme Left greeted constitutionalist women speakers with ovations enjoining them to strip. In some ways the Extreme Left could hardly be described as progressive.

From this description of what the disrupters were not some indication can be obtained of what they were. To continue this enquiry into the characters of the disrupters it might be helpful to consider where disruption broke out in 1968–70. The most publicized commotions fell into two main types. One type occurred at institutions like L.S.E., Keele and Sussex. They were rarely supported by anything like the mass of students. They were endemic and enervating but were so frequent as to lose much of their immediate impact value. Commotions were subject to the law of diminishing returns. The other type occurred at the more established redbricks such as Birmingham and Manchester. At these institutions disruption was supported by from a quarter to a half of the student body. In these cases there was a big explosion preceded and succeeded by long periods of quiet. Essex was an exceptional case. It managed to activate a substantial minority of its student body at least once a year.

The reason why disruption occurred so frequently in some institutions seems to be that these were the institutions most cut off from community life and pressures. It was difficult to dilute the passions of student factions. Places like Keele and Sussex were several miles from the nearest town. Most of their students lived on their premises. They could be little worlds of their own. This was also true of L.S.E. for rather different reasons. It was in the middle of London but not in a residential area. Institutions like Keele and Sussex presented peculiar problems to discipline. An attempt to discipline individual students could occasion a mass disturbance; and it was impossible to close a university with several thousand people actually living on the premises. Moreover either the police could not come in at all with safety or they would have had to come in such large numbers that the rest of the area would have suffered. Thus the disrupters of such institutions could and did do what they liked.

It is also useful to consider the subjects studied by the disrupters. Sociology and the social sciences contributed disproportionately to both the leadership and the rank and file of the disrupters at the newer institutions at L.S.E. At the redbricks this was less true. Sociology was unique in that its study encouraged both the revelatory and the utilitarian sides of education to the detriment of the assessment of fact. The utilitarian side of protest could be seen in the deep unease felt by many sociology students about their future careers. Too many sociology graduates were being produced for the good jobs available for them and many sociology students did not want to take jobs in welfare work or in teaching in under-privileged districts. Appeals for social welfare workers met with little response from sociology students in general or the Extreme Left in particular. It was not the number of sociology students at a university that influenced the extent and intensity of disruption but the concentration. There were as many sociology students at Cambridge as at Essex but at Essex their activities were not diluted. Disruption also tended to occur at institutions like Bradford which was overwhelmingly a technological university. It had a substantial minority of sociology students but very few arts students. The attitude of most science students is best indicated by the fact that although 45 per cent of Birmingham students were in the engineering and closely related departments none was among the 30 or so organizers of the sit-in. Medical students were those responsible for the removal of L.S.E. Extreme Left from the University of London Union. Students of subjects which demanded factual knowledge and promised financial security tended to be apathetic or constitutionalist in their sympathies. Sociology students were less fortunate. Good jobs were certain only for first-rate sociologists. The flooding of the job market with sociology students sharpened the contrast between the inflated hopes, political and financial, of sociology students and their likely fate. If part of the explanation for university disruption was detestation of bourgeois capitalism part was the fear of not being its beneficiaries.

Thus the subjects studied at universities in the years 1968–70 affected disruption. It may also be that those who chose social studies at 17 were the type of people who were easily influenced by novelty.

As already stated the Extreme Left was clearly divided into the leaders and the led, the active activists and the passive activists. The leaders were rarely very young. At L.S.E. they were nearly all in their mid-twenties. There was no formal election of leaders. They elected themselves and were approved by the outer section of the Extreme Left. It is fair to say that for disruption to gain a hold on the student body it had to have at least 200 supporters. This was the critical mass. Only with so many could mass hysteria be generated and maintained within the group and a climate of opinion be established within the institution. At L.S.E. the Extreme Left had not only an inner core and an outer circle amounting to about 200 but a fringe of about 400 who voted for Extreme Left candidates at union elections but rarely came to meetings. They felt it their duty to support world revolution but not if it took up much of their time. In fact many of them were not distinguishable from the 'moderates'. This suggests muddled thinking. Both the outer circle and the fringe found the pace too much and left politics for the Library in the course of the year. This pattern was the usual pattern in all disturbed institutions. The supporters of the Extreme Left are usually half-hearted and lacking in purpose. It is the task and difficulty of the inner core to find issues to activate the outer core and fill the 'moderates' with guilt if they offer opposition.

The disrupters were almost all middle class in origin and aware of their privileges. These filled them with guilt and the desire to identify, temporarily and while it involved no sacrifice, with less privileged groups. A brief period of agitation on behalf of 'the working class' gave many of the disrupters a sense of atonement for having been born in the middle class and being determined to remain in it. Loneliness and loss of identity were also pressures driving students to disruption. In their schools and families adolescents had had their identities made for them and had been recognizable individuals. Translation to the new environment of university had removed these identities. The new students were just anonymous units and had to make their own identities. This prospect, which is the normal step to adulthood, proved too much for the more fluid students. Unable to assert themselves as individuals they sought collective self-assertion. Mass hysteria was the result of individual inadequacies. It was not the desire to be individual but the desire to postpone this for a few years that contributed to student unrest. Disruption provided not only excitement but reassurance, comfort and company. It provided what the Americans call 'togetherness'. This was the basic attraction of 'solidarity'. The urge for it was an emotional need and not a political or academic weapon. When once the mood had passed it was no longer attractive. It was this hunger for the warmth of the herd that encouraged delusions of persecution. 'Gas ovens' was daubed on L.S.E. student lockers. The allegations of political spying and of attempts to bring universities to 1984, and the comparisons of university authorities with fascist governments of the 1930's were fantasies induced by the Extreme Left to weld the herd together. The Great Occupation of L.S.E. was disturbed by reports that the police were about to besiege the institution and take it by storm. Immediately the barricades went up. At Essex a meeting was swept by excitement when it was rumoured that an army of Right-wingers was going to march on the university. In both cases the students 'knew' for the moment that they were surrounded by the powers of darkness in exactly the same sense that many of the public 'knew' that they were paid by the Kremlin. The Extreme Left wanted the fear of persecution without any real danger. It wanted to be a beleaguered but safe minority in a hostile world. Imaginary persecution intensified imaginary conflict. Hysteria was deliberately induced.

The undergraduate period of the lives of the disrupters was a period taken out of real life. In this time they were able to re-enact the student myth. One might call it a modern adaptation of *The Student Prince*. By 1970 a whole body of student lore had been compiled. Disruption had its heroes and its martyrs. There had been defeats and victories. There had been villains and deserters. Methods of disruption had become traditional and formalized. The whole progress from protest to disruption to apathy had become a ritual. The heaviness of the symbolism—students portraying hope, freedom, sanity, Barclays Bank and investments in Southern Africa—was the obverse of its lack of connection with reality. Ritual became firmly entrenched and began to lose its vitality. Ceremonial burnings of the *Financial Times* and hangings in effigy of the vice-chancellor of Warwick University were typical manifestations. Ritual chants with a definite rhythm became widespread and adaptable for all suitable occasions. The weakness of such ritual was that of its very nature disruption demanded the appearance of change.

The basic process was one of rise from one peak of excitement to another culminating in a moment of tension and release and succeeded by a state of exhaustion. *Post coitum tristitia.* This cycle could take a week, a month, a term or a year. It could be repeated several times. The necessity for periods of recuperation explains why mass-supported disruption so rarely strikes the same institution two years running. The period of exhaustion and recovery usually takes a year or two. One of the contributory causes is the turnover in students. Each student's course, except for medicine and dentistry, lasts three or four years. In that time he can only take part in one set of disturbances and hope to get a reasonable degree. Thus a year or two is usually necessary for the composition of the student body to change so that a new intake or two can be activated. It must be stated that activation was in no way determined by real grievances. The disruptive mood always has preceded the convenient discovery of grievances. After periods of disruption even real grievances would not have aroused students from their apathy. Everything depended on mood. Each university community was in this respect self-contained. Emissaries and messages from other institutions could not arouse a university or college if it was not in the mood. This was clearly demonstrated in

the Hornsey and Guildford cases. Far from there being an international conspiracy there was a strong spirit of particularism. This
was best shown after the two years 1968–70 had ended when Welsh
students protested against the expansion of student numbers on
the grounds that more English students would be admitted to the
University of Wales. Messages of encouragement were ignored
except when disruption was already in progress.

It cannot therefore be maintained that the Extreme Left was
normally moved by events in the world at large or in the educational institution. It was more often moved by the desire for
hysteria for the sake of hysteria and without consequences. It
is safe to say that L.S.E. provided the most frequent and the most
dramatic displays of this hysteria. Students' union meetings were
made memorable by hysteria if by nothing else. It was partly the
dislike of having such scenes recorded that made the Extreme
Left begin meetings with proposals that the Press should be
excluded. Philosophically accepting that noise from the Extreme
Left would drown speeches made by the opposition successive
presidents of the union had microphones installed. A meeting was
normally preceded by a warm-up. Red flags were waved. There
were occasionally renderings of 'We all live in the red L.S.E.'.
When the meeting opened there were messages of solidarity from
the unions or other institutions. There were often appeals and
collections on behalf of various progressive causes. Sometimes a
trade unionist would come and wish the students well. Sometimes
the one porter sympathetic to disruption came to say how much
solidarity he as a member of the working class felt with those who
worked five hours a day in the Library. Appeals were made for
physical assistance to squatters and financial assistance to people
convicted for political offences. Eventually the proposal for direct
action would be made in a speech drawing together the iniquities
of imperialism, the number of directorships held by the governors
of L.S.E. and the subject of the proposal. Each ritual phrase was
greeted with ritual cheers. A higher peak of excitement was
reached when the opponents of 'direct action' spoke in face of
howls, obscenities, jeers, paper-darts, empty coca-cola tins and
many other expressions of disapproval. People jumped up and
down shaking their fists. Sometimes they surged towards the
platform. It is hardly too much to say that the Extreme Left

seemed to suffer and enjoy a collective fit of delirium. It was sometimes less the speakers for 'direct action' than those against it which gave the Extreme Left its climax. Once the meeting was over the mood changed. Of 355 who voted successfully for an occupation in March 1969 less than a tenth stayed the night. The other nine-tenths clearly felt that their duty had been done.

It was the difficulty of maintaining hysteria that made the leaders of the Extreme Left switch its apparent objects with such bewildering rapidity. Vietnam, Greece, Rhodesia, gates and discipline succeeded one another not to weaken bourgeois capitalism or London University but to maintain the dynamism and cohesion of the Socialist Society. At Bristol the issue had to be 'drummed up'. At Birmingham on the issue of representation the president of the union said, 'Although the letter of many of the student negotiations has been respected, the spirit has not. In terms of quantity it is true to say we have got a lot, but in terms of quality we have got very little indeed.' The president's ground for this criticism was that students would be given places without votes on committees. Since students would not have been in a majority on any of these committees the president's reason was not very substantial. However it ensured that students could still have an occasion for commotion. The aim of disruption was disruption.

The aim of disturbance was a state of hysteria, a sense of striving against something and a condition of self-importance through self-escape. The hysteria had to be morally and legally licensed. What ideology did was to provide a nice reason for being nasty.

Underneath, however, the disrupters all knew that their involvement in disruption was only temporary. They performed the rite and went away. Because they did not take it seriously they wished to escape responsibility for it. Knowing that at 30 they would be settled into careers they wished no record to be kept of their youthful excesses. This is why they insisted on the collective nature of responsibility. Individual members of Oxford Extreme Left refused to present themselves for disciplinary hearings on the grounds that their actions had been sanctioned by a general assembly which was therefore collectively responsible. Since no general assembly or union meeting could be exactly reconstituted the body sanctifying an act of violence was immune. It is not only principle that made disruptive groups have no official executive but the fear that such officials might be held legally responsible for acts of violence. When responsibility was collective it was non-existent. To some legal immunity from the consequences of their own actions or votes meant also moral immunity. If 200 people did something wrong and could not be punished for it each one felt absolved of any personal guilt or shame. One person hitting a policeman was doing something wrong; 200 attacking the police were doing something right.

It all ends with university life. On November 10, 1968 there was a letter in the *News of the World*.

In last Sunday's 'Student Plot' feature you stated that I am currently in charge of influence in the National Union of Students for the Radical Students' Alliance. This is not true. From 1965 to 1967 I was N.U.S. vice-president and during this period I fully supported the progressive educational demands of R.S.A. However, I have been out of all this since I left the student world and, as a tax-payer and a rate-payer, hope that the radical students will succeed without violence in revolutionising their colleges.

I I

The Basic Cause

IT IS often alleged that the 'revolt of youth' is a new phenomenon. It is alleged that it is the symptom of a sick society and that if society were different there would be less or no unrest.

The problem is permanent and all solutions are the products of circumstance. The problem is that there is in males a period between physical maturation and the gaining and acceptance of the real responsibilities of manhood. There is an excess of energy over suitable opportunities for its expenditure—a disparity increased by the sporadic nature of this energy. During the period between childhood and manhood boys often feel insecure as individuals. The problems of a change of role in society seem at times insuperable. This does not affect girls so much as their role is the same throughout life in almost all societies. This role is that of pleasing men in order to be supported and protected by them. This is why movements have largely masculine leaderships even though they may have a large number of female followers. The problem is one of what to do with unsettled young men whose personal doubts, often springing from a well-justified sense of personal inadequacy, drive them to congregate in large groups which can commit acts of anti-social behaviour without much fear of having to take responsibility for them. The period varies with historical circumstance and in some centuries life is so violent and dislocated that the 'revolt of youth' as such does not stand out. The length of the period can depend on the age at which the responsibilities of manhood are assumed. In the Ancient World the period tended to be shorter because men were assumed to become adult early; indeed until relatively modern times this was usually the case as life was too short to allow the luxury of a long adolescence. In the Dark Ages of Western Europe violence was so widespread that 'youth' was not particularly associated with it. In a sense only relatively stable and civilized societies have been able to indulge in and suffer the 'revolt of youth'.

The problem can be partly solved by encouraging the temporary self-exclusion of boys from the rest of society. In some tribal societies special quarters have been provided for unmarried men. In Sparta boys from 13 to 18 lived in special groups. Impulses towards anti-social behaviour were channelled. Food was rationed and boys were expected to go out and steal what they needed. This segregation from the rest of society had its merits. The English public school was not dissimilar in its containment and tacit condonation of the aggression of young boys. When this segregation is not maintained officially it appears unofficially and is subject to less control. The urge towards protective conformity is satisfied by the establishment of groups centred on everything from a religious faith to a football team and the members of such groups usually make great efforts to appear, both in clothing and behaviour, indistinguishable from the rest of their group. The fact that such people can choose their uniforms gives them the illusion of choice and individuality.

Those most susceptible to these impulses to anonymity and violence are those in whom other impulses and capacities are weak and who lead dull lives. The dullness of their lives is not necessarily the fault of a political, educational or social system. Some people are naturally dull—and it is in their unsettled adolescence that they are most likely both to feel and to fight it. Anti-social behaviour is commoner in the stupid than the clever and in the unoccupied than in the occupied. Those who cannot concentrate on a book can always break a window.

The adolescent gang has certain well-defined characteristics. It is unorganized but exclusive, linked by a set of slogans against a hostile world. It is aimless except when activated by hysteria. It is based on the drive for cohesion and assurance of group membership. It is these drives and the temptation to unpunished violence that causes disturbance usually attributed to the ostensible causes of dissension. In Justinian's Byzantium two chariot teams, called respectively the Green and the Blue, became identified with differing views on the nature of God. Various gangs of youthful adherents of these two groups went round the city cutting off the heads of passers-by. Fortunately manners have on the whole softened since then. There have been many spiritual successors to these factions. One has only to think of the 'sturdy apprentices' in the Middle Ages or the pastoureaux of early fourteenth century France. The latter present some interesting features. They were groups of young people who wanted to force Philip V to lead them on crusade. Philip V refused. There were great disturbances, leading on one occasion to Philip's being besieged, and the movement, which had attracted an ever larger proportion of brigands, disintegrated into violence and was bloodily suppressed. These were basically large-scale demonstrations, provided with a religious aspect, of the same impulses which in Athens helped Euripides to use material for his plays. *Ion* is based on the youthful indiscretion of a prince. Terence, the Roman playwright, also used the condoned acts of violence of boys for his plots. Whether gangs of adolescents are large or small, whether they claim to be moved by objective and idealistic impulses or admit that they like violence for its own sake, their essential natures are not different. The idealism of youth is often a synonym for its insecurity and the nastiness that this is held to condone because it is difficult to do anything about it. The combination of self-escape and self-assertion is difficult to resist for some. The combination of a belief that one is justified and immune from punishment with a belief that one is somehow elect, daring and special is also tempting. Boys can tell themselves that they are doing both right and wrong. They can tell themselves that they are opposing and mocking society when what they really mean is that they are not yet ready to enter society as adults.

It is often alleged that students are progressive influences in society. This is alleged to be true of the *Burschenschaften* of Germany after 1815. If nationalism is a progressive force then they were probably progressive. It must be stressed that the one thing student factions and youthful disrupters have never been is liberal in the modern sense of the word. The particular characteristic of violent youthful gangs is extremism.

During this century the 'revolt of youth' has more often been Right-wing than Left-wing. The universities of the Weimar Republic were overwhelmingly Right-wing. The young officers of

Japan in the 1920's and the 1930's staged abortive Right-wing revolts. No section of inter-war Rumanian society was more anti-semitic than the students. A student assembly demanded death for Carol II's Jewish mistress. In Britain things were milder, the most energetic opponents of the General Strike included students. It was students who most vigorously resisted the extension of university education to women. The famous proposal carried by Oxford Union in 1933 to the effect it would not fight for 'King and Country' shocked by its unexpectedness. It was, as events proved, not representative of the feeling of 'youth'.

The problem has become more acute this century. The principal reason is the fall in child mortality. This means that the proportion of young people in the population has risen. In industrialized countries, half the population is under 27. This means that the disruptive minority is proportionately larger in the population and thus is more difficult to control. The advent of the Welfare State has created difficulties as well as solved them and some of these difficulties are apparent at every football match and student riot. Humanitarians had previously supposed that a liberal and per-missive society would remove stresses, tensions and frictions. What they did not allow for was that many people need these conflicts and if these conflicts are not provided by external pressures they will be generated by those who wish to have them. A society in which there is relatively little hostile pressure and in which considerable efforts are made to provide opportunity and security deprives many people of the former excuses for failure. Such a deprivation is more likely to stimulate than remove bitterness.

Of recent years people have had more leisure than ever before. This is true of all levels of society. Time has to be filled in some-how. An outlet for aggression has to be found. In the under-privileged sections of the community the answer is sometimes Paki-bashing and sometimes football riots. In universities it is often the onslaught on bourgeois capitalism, liberal democracy, the university authorities etc. These targets all provide foci for hatred and aggression. It must be said that all adolescent groups like this choose as their opponents those whom they outnumber or whom they can provoke or can attack without retaliation. When punished such boys often seem genuinely aggrieved. The meaninglessness of these conflicts is seen in their disappearance or weakening when the boys reach adulthood. The victory of Arsenal and the fall of capitalism are less important to a family man of 30 than a skinhead or student of 18.

In other societies the segregation and half-toleration of the excesses of boys have sometimes been insufficient to solve the problem. In these cases a powerful impulse is given to provide a focus for aggression outside the community. Thucydides wrote that before the Peloponnesian War Athens was not entirely displeased by the prospect of war. There had not been a major war for some time and 'there were many young men'. The same train of thought was apparent in nineteenth-century Germany when Treitschke described over-long periods of peace as periods of corruption. Sometimes, as in the 1930's in Germany, the immediate aggression has been turned against a defenceless minority within the state. Boys in these situations do not think of the long-term consequences of their actions. The boys who joined the S.A. in 1932 did not take seriously the thought that they might be required to die slowly and unpleasantly in Stalingrad in order to realize the projects unmistakably outlined in *Mein Kampf*. They joined for the immediate excitement and the pleasure of beating people up. They knew also that the fear of being called unpatriotic would undermine the opponents of such activities.

A sense of guilt at opposing the actions of 'youth' has hampered the opponents of extremists' philosophies which temporarily attract youthful drifters. This sense of guilt was apparent in the 1930's and it is apparent now. This sense of guilt has been sharpened by declining respect for age. In centuries which had high death rates, to reach the age of 40 was an indication of unusual vitality and cleverness. In the Welfare State middle age is no longer an achievement in itself. It has become, indeed, to many, something to be apologized for. The stain is, for them, only removed by identifying themselves with 'youth'. All these tendencies have acquired fresh vigour in this country through the admission to universities of people who are not capable of doing the work with reasonable ease. The extension of university education to an excessively large proportion of the population has been the catalyst of disruption. If people so unfamiliar with the written word that they find it difficult to spell 'anarchy', 'governor', 'imperialism', etc. are allowed into universities to do courses on politics, economics and sociology without the sure prospect of comfortable jobs then disruption is more than likely.

Thus present-day university disruption in this country is the local and contemporary manifestation of a permanent social problem. This problem is that in every generation there is a minority, usually minute, which seeks oblivion and release in anti-social behaviour, the chief aim of which is to provide a sense of importance. What has happened in this century and become very obvious in the two years 1968–70 is that society is less willing to admit that there are unpleasant streaks inherent in human nature and that some human behaviour is irrational. Society cannot offer either an external enemy or an internal minority as scapegoat. Thus it is slowly being compelled to allow that if 'the young' are being revolutionary there must be something wrong with what they are allegedly protesting against. Even when the alleged grievance has palpably no substance some people feel obscurely guilty at saying so. It is very difficult for some progressive humanitarians to admit that the fault might be in the individual rather than the environment. Original virtue is as tempting, absolute and irrational a doctrine as original sin.

Every system has these problems. Whatever the environment disrupters disrupt. No change of system and no alteration in the structure of society would change this impulse. The guise, place and extent of disruption might change but its essential quality does not. British universities have been unlucky.

12

Conclusion

THUS THE intellectual claims and the alleged grievances of the Extreme Left should not be taken too seriously. It is rarely that they coincide with real causes for discontent. University authorities should face this unpalatable fact.

The danger behind university disruption does not lie in any possibility of revolution or of Right-wing reaction. The danger lies in the softening of will and confusion of mind in the face of mob hysteria. It lies in the willingness to justify or condone hysteria and violence. It lies in the reluctance to insist that universities should remain what they have so recently become—institutions based on the search for truth, or at least accuracy. Universities are places in which facts are accumulated and assessed logically in the hope that something will be learnt. They are the defenders of reason and it is their duty to strengthen this thin crust over the irrationality common to us all—stronger in some than others. The universities should not surrender their *raison d'être* and abdicate from their responsibilities to the community and themselves. When dispassionate and detailed examination of the grievances and demands of the advocates of 'student power' indicates that they have no real justification universities should not delude themselves into the belief that concession will buy peace without harming the universities. They should realize that what the Extreme Left wants is not participation or power but a state of demand.

What happened in the years 1968–70 was that many people in universities lost faith in the overriding need for reason. They began to suppose that revelation might be a surer source of light. They mistook destructiveness for vitality. They behaved like the Right-wing university teachers in inter-war Germany—teachers who had mildly commented 'youthful exuberance' on the excesses of National Socialist students. Even some of the victims of the Extreme Left felt some touch of guilt at condemning it. Lord Robbins put some of the blame for the misbehaviour of L.S.E. students on the failure of British politics to provide colour and described British political leaders as 'utterly second rate and uninspiring enough to fill the younger generation with disquiet and disgust'. He maintained that 'the younger generation in the West has quite a lot to worry about in general'. Some might think that the leaders of our political parties were moderate, honourable and competent men. Some might say, like one of L.S.E. Conservatives, that the basic trouble was a lack of real grievances. Many people seemed to stop expecting students to be rational and yet to concede what they demanded in their capacity as members of universities. They no longer insisted on a reasonable case or a logical presentation. This widening and deepening current within universities began to sap their moral as well as their intellectual authority. In no way is this faltering more closely shown than in the issue of freedom of speech. Academically universities were in favour of allowing Mr. Powell to address meetings at their institutions but most were not prepared to insist that he had the right to come and by the end of two years Conservative Associations were blamed for inviting Mr. Powell more than the Extreme Left were blamed for disrupting his meetings.

Student participation in all university decisions—which would in practice mean a compromise of sorts between the 'moderates' and the Extreme Left—should be resisted for several reasons. In the first place it would not be possible to make it effective. Apathy would strangle it at birth. Judging by previous experience the Extreme Left would on minute polls be the student representatives. No one can have any illusions about what they would do if they sat on committees selecting staff or deciding the content of courses. Since it is the declared aim of the Extreme Left to abolish examinations and gradings it is easy to see what would happen to the academic standards and reputations of British universities. It may be that the Extreme Left dislikes examinations because examinations have to be done by individuals. It will be objected that a minority of students on such vital committees would not be able to dominate them. However this attempt at compromise would be denounced as 'tokenism' and would provide occasion for more demands.

It would be easy to put student claims to extensive participation in university management to the test. Students sitting on staff-student committees should be elected on a 50 per cent poll. If the poll is not reached the office should remain vacant. Every student voting for a proposal should be able to make out a case for it either in speech or writing. 200 clear, factual and well-argued essays would be more convincing intellectually than a riot. Before any proposal is taken seriously by university authorities it should have gone through three union meetings with roughly constant voting figures. There should be only one union meeting a week. Union cards should be produced at union meetings in order to exclude non-students. Students should have a right to contract out of students' unions. In fact it might be possible for each university to have two students' unions, one for the management of facilities and one for politics. An element of direct responsibility should be introduced by the freezing of official union funds for political and legal purposes. When proposals for financial assistance to students charged with breaking the law and to political organizations outside the university are carried, only those present and in favour should be expected to contribute. The quorum for union meetings could, if students are sure they wish to participate in running the university, safely be raised to 10 per cent of the student body. The expectation that students should be responsible for what they do should be encouraged by having some representative posts filled by random selection from among those who voted for the institution of maintenance or the posts. Refusal to take up the posts could mean small fines. Such methods would soon show the extent and intensity of student desire for real power in their universities. Neither the Extreme Left nor the 'moderates' could reasonably object. The individual student must be made to feel responsible for his own actions and to consider their implications before he performs them.

It must be realized and asserted that universities stand for independence and variety of thought and that those who by disruption attack these principles should be expelled. There is no middle way, despite the spasmodic assertions of the 'moderates'. If universities do not accept the challenge they will find themselves gradually mutated into centres of sterile anarchy. Such a development would certainly change society for the worse. Dead universities would mean a nastier society. The end of our universities as we have come to have them this century would mean the end of one of our worthiest if most recently established traditions.

Index

Aberystwyth University College, 30, 36, 79, 85, 86

Adams, Dr. Walter, 20, 29, 32, 34, 36, 41–4, 84, 139, 156

Allsop, Kenneth, 23

Amery, Julian, M.P., 73

Anderson, Hugh, 38, 69, 80, 96

Annan, Lord, 95, 137

Architectural Association School, 103

Armstrong, Sir William, 70

Arnold, 53

Ashby, Sir Eric, 16, 74

Association of Education Committees, 24, 38

— of Municipal Corporations, 24

— of Teachers in Technical Colleges, 40–1, 50, 53, 104

— of University Teachers, 28, 40–41, 45, 82, 104, 136

Aston University, 68, 91, 128

Atkinson, Norman, M.P., 52

Bains, Ald. Lawrence, 52, 54

Barber, Anthony, M.P., 109

Barclays Bank, 89–90, 97, 109, 161

Barnes, Winston, 28

Bath University, 60, 61

Beeching, Lord, 43, 68, 120, 131

Belfast University, 85

Bell, Ronald, M.P., 59, 72, 131

Biafra, 2, 27, 62

Biggs-Davison, John, M.P., 67

Birmingham College of Commerce, 92

— College of Education, 19

— *Mail*, 126, 148

— *Post*, 112, 148, 151

— University, 21, 25–6, 63, 66, 69, 92, 102, 106, 108, 112–17, 120–1, 126, 128, 135–6, 139, 143, 155, 157–8, 163

'Black Papers', 39, 46, 74, 85, 109

Bolton College of Art, 100

— Institute of Technology, 100

— Technical Colleges, 86

Borough Polytechnic, 32

Bournemouth College of Technology, 23

Bowden, Lord, 84, 90–1

Boyle, Sir Edward, M.P., 42, 128

Bradford University, 36–7, 62, 66, 71, 94, 101, 123, 134, 139, 158

Braine, John, 127

Brandreth, Giles, 45

Brazil, 12

Briggs, Prof. Asa, 69, 135, 137

Bristol University, 3, 25–6, 33, 37, 45, 66, 114–16, 135, 139, 163

British Council of Churches, 151

F